WHAT YOU NEED TO KNOW ABOUT

THE HOLY SPIRIT

IN 12 LESSONS

MAX ANDERS

THOMAS NELSON PUBLISHERS
Nashville

© 1995 by Max Anders

Published in Nashville, Tennessee, by Thomas Nelson, Inc.

All rights reserved. Written permission must be secured from the publisher to use or reproduce any part of this book except for brief quotations in critical reviews or articles.

Unless otherwise indicated, Scripture quotations are from the *New King James Version of the Bible*, © 1979, 1980, 1982, 1990, Thomas Nelson, Inc., Publishers.

Scripture quotations identified by NASB are from the *New American Standard Bible*, © 1960, 1962, 1963, 1968, 1971, 1973, 1975, 1977, by the Lockman Foundation, and used by permission.

Scripture quotations identified by NIV are from the *Holy Bible, New International Version*, © 1973, 1978, 1984 by International Bible Society, and used by permission of Zondervan Bible Publishers.

Scripture quotations identified by PHILLIPS are from *The New Testament in Modern Speech: Revised Edition*, © 1972 by Macmillan, and used by permission.

Scripture quotations identified by LB are from *The Living Bible*, © 1971 by Tyndale House Publishers, and used by permission.

Scripture quotations from *The Holy Bible, New Century Version* copyright © 1987, 1988, 1991 by Word Publishing, Dallas, Texas, and used by permission.

Library of Congress Cataloging-in-Publication Data

Anders, Max E., 1947–
    The Holy Spirit / Max Anders.
    Includes bibliographical references.
    ISBN 0-7852-1347-3
    1. Holy Spirit.   I. Title.   II. Series.
  BT121.2.A52   1995
  231'.3—dc20   95–42822
                                                                      CIP

Printed in the United States of America

1 2 3 4 5 6 7 8 — 00 99 98 97

Contents

Introduction to the *What You Need to Know Series*   iv

How To Teach This Book   vi

Chapter 1   Who Is the Holy Spirit?   1

Chapter 2   What Does the Holy Spirit Do?   12

Chapter 3   What Is the Role of the Holy Spirit
in My Salvation?   26

Chapter 4   How Does the Holy Spirit Help Me?   44

Chapter 5   How Does the Holy Spirit Change Me?   57

Chapter 6   How Does the Holy Spirit Use Me?   74

Chapter 7   Are Signs and Wonders Valid for Today?   87

Chapter 8   What Does It Mean to Be Filled
with the Holy Spirit?   104

Chapter 9   What Is the Unpardonable Sin?   119

Chapter 10   How Do I Respond to the Holy Spirit?   131

Chapter 11   What Is the Fruit of the Spirit? (Part One)   144

Chapter 12   What Is the Fruit of the Spirit? (Part Two)   159

Bibliography   175

Master Review   177

About the Author   183

Introduction to the
What You Need to Know Series

You hold in your hands a tool with enormous potential—the ability to help ground you, and a whole new generation of other Christians, in the basics of the Christian faith.

I believe the times call for just this tool. We face a serious crisis in the church today . . . namely, a generation of Christians who know the truth but who do not live it. An even greater challenge is coming straight at us, however: a coming generation of Christians who may not even know the truth!

Many Christian leaders agree that today's evangelical church urgently needs a tool flexible enough to be used by a wide variety of churches to ground current and future generations of Christians in the basics of Scripture and historic Christianity.

This guide, and the whole series from which it comes—the *What You Need to Know* series, can be used by individuals or groups for just that reason.

Here are five other reasons why we believe you will enjoy using this guide:

1. It is easy to read.

You don't want to wade through complicated technical jargon to try to stumble on the important truths you are looking for. This series puts biblical truth right out in the open. It is written in a warm and friendly style, with even a smattering of humor here and there. See if you don't think it is different from anything you have ever read before.

2. It is easy to teach.

You don't have time to spend ten hours preparing for Sunday school, small group, or discipleship lessons. On the other hand, you don't want watered down material that insults your group's intellect. There is real meat in these pages, but it is presented in a way that is easy to teach. It follows a question-and-answer format that can be used to cover the material, along with discussion questions at the end of each chapter that make it easy to get group interaction going.

3. It is thoroughly biblical.

You believe the Bible, and don't want to use anything that isn't thoroughly biblical. This series has been written and reviewed by a team of people who are well-educated, personally committed Christians who have a high view of Scripture, and great care has been taken to reflect what the Bible teaches. If the Bible is unambiguous on a subject, such as the resurrection of Christ, then that subject is presented unambiguously.

4. It respectfully presents differing evangelical positions.

You don't want anyone forcing conclusions on you that you don't agree with. There are many subjects in the Bible on which there is more than one responsible position. When that is the case, this series presents those positions with respect, accuracy and fairness. In fact, to make sure, a team of evaluators from various evangelical perspectives has reviewed each of the volumes in this series.

5. It lets you follow up with your own convictions and distinctives on a given issue.

You may have convictions on an issue that you want to communicate to the people to whom you are ministering. These books give you that flexibility. After presenting the various responsible positions that may be held on a given subject, you will find it easy then to identify and expand upon your view, or the view of your church.

We send this study guide to you with the prayer that God may use it to help strengthen His church for her work in these days.

How To Teach This Book

The books in this series are written so that they can be used as a thirteen-week curriculum, ideal for Sunday school classes or other small-group meetings. You will notice that there are only twelve chapters—to allow for a session when you may want to do something else. Every quarter seems to call for at least one different type of session, because of holidays, summer vacation, or other special events. If you use all twelve chapters, and still have a session left in the quarter, have a fellowship meeting with refreshments, and use the time to get to know others better. Or use the session to invite newcomers in hopes they will continue with the course.

All ten books in the series together form a "Basic Knowledge Curriculum" for Christians. Certainly Christians would eventually want to know more than is in these books, but they should not know less. Therefore, the series is excellent for seekers, for new Christians, and for Christians who may not have a solid foundation of biblical education. It is also a good series for those whose biblical education has been spotty.

Of course, the books can also be used in small groups and discipleship groups. If you are studying the book by yourself, you can simply read the chapters and go through the material at the end. If you are using the books to teach others, you might find the following guidelines helpful:

Teaching Outline

1. Begin the session with prayer.

2. Consider having a quiz at the beginning of each meeting over the self-test from the chapter to be studied for that day. The quiz can be optional, or the group may want every-

one to commit to it, depending on the setting in which the material is taught. In a small discipleship group or one-on-one, it might be required. In a larger Sunday school class, it might need to be optional.

3. At the beginning of the session, summarize the material. You may want to have class members be prepared to summarize the material. You might want to bring in information that was not covered in the book. There might be some in the class who have not read the material, and this will help catch them up with those who did. Even for those who did read it, a summary will refresh their minds and get everyone into a common mind-set. It may also generate questions and discussion.

4. Discuss the material at the end of the chapters as time permits. Use whatever you think best fits the group.

5. Have a special time for questions and answers, or encourage questions during the course of discussion. If you are asked a question you can't answer (it happens to all of us), just say you don't know, but that you will find out. Then, the following week, you can open the question and answer time, or perhaps the discussion time, with the answer to the question from last week.

6. Close with prayer.

You may have other things you would like to incorporate, and flexibility is the key to success. These suggestions are given only to guide, not to dictate. Prayerfully, choose a plan suited to your circumstances.

The Holy Spirit is stronger than genius.
■ Martin Luther

Who Is the Holy Spirit?

If you're like me, you might need a little "brushing up" on your knowledge of our solar system. There are nine planets that orbit our sun. Starting with the planet closest to the sun and moving away, we have Mercury, Venus, Earth, Mars, Jupiter, Saturn, Uranus, Neptune, and Pluto.

In one of my other books, I used one variation of an illustration to convey the enormous size of our solar system (*30 Days to Understanding the Bible* 13–14). I first heard this illustration from Chuck Swindoll years ago.

Imagine you are in the middle of the Bonneville Salt Flats in Utah, with nothing but tabletop flat ground around you for miles. There you put down a beach ball two feet in diameter, which will represent the sun. To get a feel for the immensity of the solar system, walk about a city block and put down an ordinary BB for the first planet, Mercury.

Go another block and, for Venus, put down a small pea. Step off yet another block and put down a regular green pea, for Earth. Go a final city block from there and, for Mars, put down another, small pea. Then sprinkle some grass seed around for an asteroid belt.

We have now walked about four blocks, and we have a beach ball (sun), BB (Mercury), small pea (Venus), a regular pea (Earth), another small pea (Mars), and grass seed (asteroid belt). Now things really begin to stretch out.

Continue for another quarter of a mile. Place an orange on the ground for Jupiter. Walk another third of a mile and put down a golf ball for Saturn. Now lace up your tennis shoes and check their tread. Then step off another *mile* and, for Uranus, drop a marble. Go *another* mile and place a cherry there for Neptune. Finally, walk for *another* two miles and put down another BB for Pluto. Pluto is way, way out there!

Now go up in an airplane and look down. On a smooth surface

almost ten miles in diameter, we have a beach ball, a BB, a small pea, a regular pea, another small pea, some grass seed, an orange, a golf ball, a marble, a cherry, and another BB. A lot of space, and only a few tiny objects!

I have learned something unusual about Pluto, our most distant planet. At the time it was discovered, no telescope was powerful enough to see it. Astronomer Percival Lowell began searching from his private observatory in Flagstaff, Arizona, for an unknown planet at the far edge of our solar system. He had noticed that something unseen seemed to be influencing Uranus, the most distant planet known to us at that time. He concluded that the only thing that could be making Uranus act in such a way was if another heavenly body were exercising gravitational pull on it. He concluded that there must be another planet out there, so far away that it was as yet unseen. Some time later, his computations and deductions were vindicated when the planet was finally seen by Clyde W. Tombaugh on February 18, 1930, verifying what Lowell had suspected.

In this chapter we learn that. . .

1. The Scriptures reveal the Holy Spirit to be a person, with all the characteristics of a living, personal being.
2. The Scriptures reveal the Holy Spirit to be God, with all the defining characteristics of a divine being.
3. The Scriptures reveal the Holy Spirit to be on an equal level with the Father and the Son, though distinct from them in role.

Discovering Pluto is a bit like learning about the Holy Spirit. We cannot see Him, but we know of His presence because of the undeniable influence He exerts. He didn't walk the earth, as Jesus of Nazareth did. He is not the main focus of people of all faiths who believe in God. Indeed, many who believe in God do not believe in the Holy Spirit. The only way we conclude that a Holy Spirit exists is through the teachings of Scripture and experience.

Who is the Holy Spirit? To some, He is not a person, but an impersonal force, like school spirit—religious enthusiasm, if you will. To others, He is a mystery, someone or something unknown, and, perhaps, someone or something to fear.

I remember very well the evening of September 1, 1966. It was very late, and I was sitting at the kitchen table with Jake Berger, who was telling me about Jesus and encouraging me to invite Him into my life. My greatest concern was trying to become a Christian and then not being able to pull it off. I said, "Jake, I've turned over new leaves before, and they never stayed turned over."

Jake replied, "Becoming a Christian isn't like turning over a new leaf. When you invite Christ into your life, you are born again. The Holy Spirit comes into your life and will help you live the new life Christ calls you to."

For some reason, I assumed that I ought to *feel* this happen. I imagined in my mind a Max-shaped Spirit sitting beside me, and as I prayed for Christ to save me and for the Holy Spirit to come into my life to help me become the person He wanted me to be and who I wanted to be, *I actually felt something.* What it was, I don't know, but it was extremely disconcerting. It seemed that I could feel this Max-shaped Spirit gradually slipping into me so that His outline began nearly to merge with mine, sort of like when you are focusing a camera, trying to get two identical images to merge into one. However, just as I was about to get Him completely into me, I would lose the feeling. Then I would pray louder, longer, and more intensely to try to "will" the Holy Spirit to merge with me; but He kept slipping away. I remember saying, "I've almost got Him, I've almost got Him. Oh, no, He's slipping away!" Jake tried to convince me that I might not feel anything, but I left that night feeling frustrated and not sure I was a Christian.

Why I need to know who the Holy Spirit is:

1. In order to be true to the teachings of Scripture, I need to understand who the Holy Spirit is.
2. Since He is God, I need to give Him the recognition, worship, and praise that God deserves.
3. If I do not know who the Holy Spirit is, I will not enjoy a proper relationship with Him or have His full ministry in my life.

Now, after nearly thirty years of being a Christian, I realize my concept of the Holy Spirit and His role in my salvation was based on some faulty assumptions. In spite of it all, Jesus saved me that night; the Holy Spirit came into my life that night and took pity on me, straightening out my major misconceptions over the next several years. Only heaven will get us completely straightened out. My own experience, plus twenty years in the ministry, has convinced me, however, that many of us need a few things tied down when it comes to our understanding of the Holy Spirit.

In this book, we are going to try to tie down the major loose ends of our understanding about the Holy Spirit. In doing so, we are going to try to say all the Bible says about the Holy Spirit, but we are going to try equally hard not to say *more* than the Bible says about the Holy Spirit. I don't have enough confidence in my own ability to produce "ideas" about the Holy Spirit. I'm going to stick with the Bible. In this chapter, we want to begin with the basics, answering three questions.

Why Believe the Holy Spirit Is a Person?

The Scriptures reveal the Holy Spirit to be a person, with all the characteristics of a living, personal being.

My brother and his wife had two children early in their marriage—a boy and a girl. On the birth of his third child, my brother quipped, "Well, I always said I wanted three children—one of each: a he, a she, and an it." His tongue was firmly in his cheek. We all got a good laugh out of it, though a couple of grandmothers didn't see the humor in it. However, thirteen years later, somewhere around his fortieth birthday, he became the father of a fourth child, so his whole "plan" collapsed.

(The "it," by the way, went on to be an outstanding athlete, musician, and scholar, graduating from a prestigious college magna cum laude and Phi Beta Kappa. In that sense, he did get an "it." No one else in our family, male or female, has come close to that kind of academic achievement. We were all very proud of *her!* An uncle's pride [and family harmony] requires me to mention that the other three children are outstanding, too! I just wanted you to know that the "it" turned out just fine.)

The Holy Spirit is a person, not an "it."

Much as my brother wanted "a he, a she, and an it," many people see God, in the Trinity, as a *He*, a *He*, and an *It*. I suspect the problem goes back to the King James translation of the Bible. *God* is a masculine word in the original language of the Bible, *Jesus* is a masculine word, but *Spirit* is a neuter word, a concept rather foreign to English. The word is literally "breath" or "wind," though it was also translated "spirit" or "ghost" in A.D. 1611 when the King James Bible was translated. As a result, the King James Version refers to the Holy Spirit as "it." This, plus general theological uncertainty about the Holy Spirit, has caused some to be confused as to whether He is a real person. He is, of course, and many of the more recent translations of the Bible refer to Him as "He" rather than "It," helping to dispel the impression created by the King James Version.

One key reason why we believe in the "personality" of the Holy Spirit is that He has the characteristics of a person. He has intellect, emotion, and will. An example of His "intellect" is found in 1 Corinthians 2:10–11, where the Spirit is said to "know the things of God." As hard as the brightest among us struggle to know the things of God, we would have to admit that if the Holy Spirit knows the mind of God (the Father), He must have intellect. An example of His "emotions" is found in Ephesians 4:30, where we read that it is possible to grieve the Holy Spirit. You cannot grieve an impersonal force. Finally, an example of His "will" is found in 1 Corinthians 12:11, where we read that the Holy Spirit gives spiritual gifts "as He wills."

In addition to His possessing the characteristics of personhood—intellect, emotion, and will—the Holy Spirit does things that only a person would do. The Holy Spirit teaches us, He prays for us, He performs miracles, He comforts us and guides us. These are things a *person*, not an impersonal force, would do. And though the word *spirit* is neuter in the original language of the Bible, sometimes when a pronoun is used to refer to the Holy Spirit, the pronoun *He* is used (John 16:13–14) instead of the expected *It*. This was no mistake on the part of the writers of the Bible. It was a deliberate reference to the Holy Spirit as a person.

Today, those who do not believe the Holy Spirit is a person usually believe that He is merely a force emanating from God the Father. This position can be held only by mentally ripping some verses out of your Bible, pretending they aren't there. A high view of *all* of Scripture will lead a person unfailingly to the conclusion that the Holy Spirit is a person.

Why Believe the Holy Spirit Is God?

The Scriptures reveal the Holy Spirit to be God, with all the defining characteristics of a divine being.

Saying that the Holy Spirit is a person does not say that He is God. Yet, there is ample additional evidence in Scripture to verify that He is divine. The most direct is found in Acts 5:3–4. Two converted Jews, Ananias and his wife, Sapphira, sold a piece of land they owned and brought the proceeds of the sale to give to the fledgling church in Jerusalem. They kept some of the money for themselves and gave the rest to the apostle Peter. However, they apparently lied to Peter, telling him that they were giving all the proceeds of the sale of the land to the church. Perhaps they wanted to make themselves look more spiritual. Peter learned of their deception and said, "Ananias, why has Satan filled your heart to lie to the Holy Spirit and keep back part of the price of the land for yourself? While it remained, was it not your own? And after it was sold, was it not in your own control? Why have you conceived this thing in your heart? You have not lied to men but to God." Peter declares that to lie to the Holy Spirit is to lie to God.

In addition, the Holy Spirit has three defining characteristics of God: He is all-knowing (omniscient), all-powerful (omnipotent), and everywhere simultaneously (omnipresent). We see His omniscience in 1 Corinthians 2:10–11, "God has **The Holy Spirit has** revealed them to us through His Spirit. For the **divine** Spirit searches all things, yes, the deep things of **characteristics.** God. For what man knows the things of a man except the spirit of the man which is in him? Even so no one knows the things of God except the Spirit of God."

We read in the creation account in the first chapter of Genesis that the Spirit participated with God in the creation of the world, implying His omnipotence.

Finally, concerning the omnipresence of the Spirit, the writer of many of the psalms, King David, wrote, "Where can I go from Your Spirit? Or where can I flee from Your presence? If I ascend into heaven, You are there; if I make my bed in hell [Sheol, the netherworld], behold, You are there" (Psalm 139:7–8).

The Holy Spirit was responsible for the miraculous conception of Jesus, restrains sin in the world, and gives spiritual gifts to Christians. The complete evidence from Scripture leaves little doubt that the Holy Spirit is a divine person.

Why Believe the Holy Spirit Is a Member of the Trinity?

The Scriptures reveal the Holy Spirit to be on an equal level with the Father and the Son, though distinct from them in role.

When I was growing up, I had two brothers, one two years older than I and one four years older. They were always bigger than I was and knew more than I did, so I concluded that I was short and stupid. I was neither, but no one told me that. We lived in a very small town, and one day when I was about six years old and my brothers were eight and ten, the new grocery store owner asked me my name.

"Just call me Shorty," I said in dead earnestness.

As it turned out, all three of us are now either a little over or a little under six feet tall, and each of us possesses advanced knowledge in a specialized area. It was such a revelation to me when I finally realized I was not short or stupid. There is much more equality among us now that we have grown up.

A similar point is true with the Father, Son, and Holy Spirit. An immature understanding of them might conclude that God the Father is the biggest and best, Jesus is second, and the Holy Spirit brings up the rear. A more mature understanding, however, leads us to a different conclusion. Any appearance of inequality among the Father, Son, and Holy Spirit results from differences in their roles that make one more prominent than another. The differences in role, however, do not mean inequality in personhood. A husband and a wife have different roles, but before God they are equal.

> The Father, Son, and Holy Spirit are God.

As God, the Holy Spirit is the third member of the Trinity. We deal more fully with the Trinity in the first volume in this series, on the subject of "God." In historical Christian teaching, the doctrine of the Trinity states that God is one God, existing in three persons. Though the terminology gets tricky to understand, theologians and Bible teachers say God was "one God in substance but three in subsistence." Our finite minds, corrupted by the ravages of sin, cannot fully comprehend this, even though the Bible teaches it. God is three persons and yet one God. It is an "antinomy," which means, "two apparently mutually exclusive truths that must be embraced simultaneously." The truths are not really mutually exclusive, or else God would be the author of nonsense, which He isn't. But with our limited information and intellectual capacity, they *appear* mutually exclusive. With that understanding, God the Father, God the Son, and God the Holy Spirit are the three members of the Trinity.

We see the Father, Son, and Holy Spirit linked together in two key New Testament passages. In 2 Corinthians 13:14, Paul writes a benediction that includes all three: "The grace of the Lord Jesus Christ, and the love of God, and the communion [fellowship] of the Holy Spirit be with you all." If Jesus and the Holy Spirit are not God, it would be presumptuous indeed to link them in the same breath with the Father.

Furthermore, in Matthew 28:19, Jesus instructs the disciples to "Go therefore and make disciples of all the nations, baptizing them in the name [not names!] of the Father and of the Son and of the Holy Spirit." James I. Packer says, "These three persons are the one God to whom Christians commit themselves" (*Concise Theology* 41).

Not coincidentally, we find the members of the Trinity present at Jesus' baptism. Jesus is in the water, God the Father speaks from heaven, and the Holy Spirit descends on Him in the visible form of a dove (Mark 1:9–11).

Finally, we see the Trinitarian prayer for grace and peace from the Father, the Spirit, and Jesus Christ in Revelation 1:4–5. In the Trinitarian benediction, we see the Father mentioned first, the Son second, and the Spirit third. Yet in the Revelation passage, we see the Father first, the Spirit second, and the Son third. This capacity to alter the order of persons mentioned only reinforces their equality in the minds of the inspired writers of Scripture.

We see, then, taken in the whole, that there is ample evidence to believe the Holy Spirit is God, the third member of the Trinity.

Conclusion

Who is the Holy Spirit? He is the third person of the Trinity, whose role in the Godhead is less obvious to mankind than the Father and the Son but just as crucial. If we want to know God, if we want to live a vital Christian life, if we want the meaning and satisfaction of doing something deeply meaningful with our lives, if we want to understand the Scripture, if we want the ability to weather the ups and downs of life, if we want to keep a clear conscience, we need to understand who the Holy Spirit is and what His ministry is to us. We need to understand how we are to relate to Him. This subtle, behind-the-scenes Helper, Comforter, and Guide wants and needs to be a central figure in our lives. We hope that this volume will contribute to that goal. We begin by understanding that He is a person, He is God, He is the third person of the Trinity. In the name of the Father, Son, and Holy Spirit.

Speed Bump!

Slow down to be sure you've gotten the main points of this chapter.

Question
Answer

Q1. Why believe the Holy Spirit is a person?

A1. The Scriptures reveal the Holy Spirit to be a person, with all the characteristics of a *personal* being.

Q2. Why believe the Holy Spirit is God?

A2. The Scriptures reveal the Holy Spirit to be God, with all the defining characteristics of a *divine* being.

Q3. Why believe the Holy Spirit is a member of the Trinity?

A3. The Scriptures reveal the Holy Spirit to be on an *equal* level with the Father and the Son though distinct from then in role.

Fill in the Blank

Question
Answer

Q1. Why believe the Holy Spirit is a person?

A1. The Scriptures reveal the Holy Spirit to be a person, with all the _____ of a living, _____ being .

Q2. Why believe the Holy Spirit is God?

A2. The Scriptures reveal the Holy Spirit to be God, with all the defining characteristics of a living, _____ being.

Q3. Why believe the Holy Spirit is a member of the Trinity?

A3. The Scriptures reveal the Holy Spirit to be on an _____ level with the Father and the Son, though distinct from them in role.

For Further Thought and Discussion

1. What was your concept of the Holy Spirit before you read this chapter? If it has changed any, how has it changed?

2. How important do you think the Holy Spirit is in the life of most Christians? How much do you think most Christians know about Him and rely on Him on a daily basis? How much do you think it hurts the Christian to be ignorant of the Holy Spirit?

3. Do you think the Holy Spirit minds being a less conspicuous member of the Trinity? If not, why not? Do you think there are any lessons for us in observing the ministry of the Holy Spirit compared to the ministries of the Father and the Son?

What If I Don't Believe?

1. If I don't believe what I've just read about the Holy Spirit, I run counter to historic Christianity, I have some very difficult things in the Bible to explain, and I fall into the category of historic heresy.

2. If I omit one member of the Trinity, I miss out on a full relationship with God.

3. Much of the Bible will become very confusing to me, because I have to try to understand it to be teaching something about the Spirit that it is not teaching. I become susceptible to false teaching, not only about the Spirit, but all the Bible. I become vulnerable to cults and false religions.

For Further Study

1. Scripture
Several passages in the Bible are central to understanding who the Holy Spirit is. They include:

- Genesis 1: 2

- Psalm 139:7

- John 14:14–17, 23

- Acts 5:1–4

- 1 Corinthians 2:10–11

- 1 Corinthians 12:11, 14

- 2 Corinthians 13:14

- Ephesians 4:30

Read these passages and consider how they add to your understanding of who the Holy Spirit is.

2. Books
Several other books are very helpful in studying this subject. They are listed below in general order of difficulty. If I could read only one of these, I would read the first one:

Know What You Believe, Paul Little
A Survey of Bible Doctrine, Charles Ryrie
Essential Truths of the Christian Faith, R. C. Sproul
Flying Closer to the Flame, Charles Swindoll
Keep in Step with the Spirit, James I. Packer

*My own experience is that the Bible is dull
when I am dull. When I am really alive, and
set upon the text with a tidal pressure of
living affinities, it opens, it multiplies
discoveries, and reveals depths even faster
than I can note them. The worldly spirit
shuts the Bible; the Spirit of God makes it a
fire, flaming out all meanings and glorious
truths.*
■ Horace Bushnell (1802–1876)

What Does the Holy Spirit Do?

Washington, D.C., is a grand national capital. Beauty, of course, is in the eye of the beholder, but I consider it the most beautiful capital in the world. Certainly, there are other capitals that have much to commend them: Rome, with its ancient ruins and glorious climate; Paris with its Eiffel Tower, Arc de Triomphe, Seine River, and Cathedral of Notre Dame; London with its Westminster Abbey, Buckingham Palace, and Tower of London. A good case also could be made for St. Petersburg, capital of the old Russian Empire, Constantinople (Istanbul), and Vienna. You might add others.

I still prefer Washington, D.C. The city was planned. George Washington himself selected the site for the capital, which was the geographic center of the thirteen colonies. A French planner, L'Enfant, drew a master plan for the entire city before the first stone was laid. The formal section is not dirty and crowded, with ugly buildings standing right at the elbows of the beautiful buildings, the way other capitals tend to be.

The city's major attractions are laid out in a massive cross. At the base of the cross is the Capitol building. At the top of the cross is the Lincoln Memorial. A huge, narrow expanse of grass, called the Mall, stretches like a long, green carpet between the Capitol and the Lincoln Memorial. Where the arms of the cross meet the post of the cross, the Washington Monument rises the height of a 55-story building. At the far left arm of the cross lies the White House, and at the far right arm of the cross, across the tidal basin, is the Jefferson Memorial. There are many other glorious features of the city, but they all are understood in relation to these.

In the springtime, cherry trees in full bloom turn the city into a pink wonderland. An explosion of flowers punctuates all the important streets, buildings, and parks during the spring and summer, due largely to the efforts of Lady Bird Johnson some years ago. There is an air of respect as tourists wander through the memorials, the museums of the amazing Smithsonian Institution, the stupefyingly enormous Pentagon with its three and a half million square feet of office space, and the many art galleries. It is an impressive place indeed.

In this chapter we learn . . .

Four primary areas of the Holy Spirit's activity:

1. In the Old Testament, the Holy Spirit helped in creation, revealed truth to people, and empowered people to do God's will.
2. In the New Testament, the Holy Spirit empowered the ministry of Jesus and His church.
3. Today, the Holy Spirit helps Christians know, be, and do what God wants.
4. In the future, the Holy Spirit will help bring history to an end and usher in eternity.

Perhaps the most spectacular view of Washington, D.C., is from the air at night. You can see all the major sights illuminated against a backdrop of utter blackness. The White House, Capitol Building, Washington Monument, Lincoln Memorial, and Jefferson Memorial all are gleaming white, like diamonds on black velvet. Even at ground level, however, you cannot pinpoint the source of the illumination for these magnificent buildings. As you walk around the White House, for example, its stunning architectural features are highlighted perfectly with thousands of watts of light, but you cannot see the lights. They are carefully concealed by landscaping and other means.

If you could see the lights, the engineers would have failed; for the whole point of the lights is not to call attention to themselves but to highlight the buildings. It is when you give no thought to the lighting at all, and you are lost in the beauty and grandeur of the buildings, that the lighting engineers have done their best job.

So it is with the Holy Spirit. Jesus is like the buildings and monuments. The Holy Spirit is like the lighting around the buildings and monuments. The Holy Spirit's job is not to be seen but to throw light on Jesus. It is when you see Jesus most clearly that the Holy Spirit is most at work.

We are living in an age in which there is great interest in the Holy Spirit. The ascendance of the charismatic movement is the most obvious example of this, but even among evangelicals and some mainline churches there is intense interest in the Holy Spirit. Perhaps because we feel so powerless in our age of rapid change, disintegrating moral and social standards, and impersonal technology, we are drawn to the power of the Spirit of God and want to experience His power in our lives.

There is nothing wrong with this interest and desire. However, we must understand that the fundamental posture of the Holy Spirit is not to focus on Himself; it is to throw light on Jesus.

As we look more closely in this chapter, and even through the remainder of the book, we want to keep this always in mind: the Holy Spirit's focus is Jesus.

What Did the Holy Spirit Do in the Old Testament?

In the Old Testament, the Holy Spirit helped in creation, revealed truth to people, and empowered people to do God's will.

To say that the Holy Spirit's job is to focus on Jesus is true of His present ministry. We see the Holy Spirit in the Old Testament, but since Jesus is not seen until the New Testament, the role of the Holy Spirit in the Old Testament could not be to focus on Jesus. So what was it?

There are three primary tasks the Holy Spirit performed in the Old Testament. He helped create the universe, He revealed the Scripture and other truth to people, and He empowered people to do things. Let's look at each of them.

Creation

It is a little confusing to talk about who is responsible for creation, because each member of the Trinity is given credit in Scripture. In Revelation 4:11 we see God sitting on a throne in heaven, surrounded by celestial beings saying to Him, "You are worthy, O Lord, To receive glory and honor and power; For You created all things, And by Your will they exist and were created." So, in this passage, creation is attributed to God the Father.

However, take a look at Colossians 1:16, which is speaking of Jesus: "For by Him all things were created that are in heaven and that are on earth, visible and invisible, whether thrones or dominions or principalities or powers. All things were created through Him and for Him."

But the Holy Spirit is not left out of the process. In Genesis 1, we read:

"In the beginning God created the heavens and the earth. And the earth was without form, and void; and darkness was on the face of the deep. And the Spirit of God was hovering over the face of the waters."

Exactly what the Spirit was doing moving over the surface of the waters is uncertain, but the context of the entire chapter is "creation," so it seems a small jump to conclude that He was involved in the creation of the world. The role of the Spirit is often seen as related to the giving of life. Job said, "The Spirit of God has made me, and the breath of the Almighty gives me life" (Job 33:4). In another passage, speaking of animal life in the sea, the psalmist wrote, "You take away their breath, they die and return to their dust. You send forth Your Spirit, they are created; and You renew the face of the earth" (Psalm 104:29–30).

Why I need to know what the Holy Spirit does:

1. To have a proper appreciation for the Holy Spirit and an adequate capacity to worship Him.
2. To avoid falling into error concerning the ministry of the Holy Spirit.
3. To make sure I do not miss out on the Holy Spirit's ministry in my life.

God does not contradict Himself. These passages can be understood together by saying that all three members of the Trinity were involved in creation. The role of the Holy Spirit seems to have been the imparting of life, particularly when the word "spirit" and "breath" are the same word in Hebrew. When Genesis 2:7 says, "The Lord God formed man of the dust of the ground, and breathed into his nostrils the breath of life," it is not far-fetched to infer the Holy Spirit's involvement. So the Holy Spirit's role in the Old Testament included creation.

Revelation
A second activity of the Holy Spirit in the Old Testament was revealing God's truth to humanity. God's chief human instrument

for giving His message to humanity was the prophet. These were usually men who ran the gamut of society. Some were uneducated, counterculture, reclusive people, while others were refined, sophisticated, highly educated, and highly placed in society. Yet they all had one thing in common. God had chosen them to be instruments of His direct revelation that they, in turn, were responsible to communicate to God's chosen audience. The apostle Peter wrote: "No prophecy was ever made by an act of human will, but men moved by the Holy Spirit spoke from God" (2 Peter 1:21, NASB). In 2 Samuel 23:1–2, King David identifies himself as the writer of Psalms, and says, "The Spirit of the Lord spoke by me, and His word was on my tongue." So we see that the Holy Spirit was the agent who revealed God's truth to humanity through prophets and through the Scriptures.

Power

Finally, the Holy Spirit empowered people to do the will of God. When the leadership of the Israelites was being transferred from Moses to his protégé, Joshua, the Lord said to Moses, "Take Joshua the son of Nun with you, a man in whom is the Spirit, and lay your hand on him; set him before Eleazar the priest and before all the congregation, and inaugurate him in their sight. And you shall give some of your authority to him, that all the congregation of the children of Israel may be obedient" (Numbers 27:18–20).

The Holy Spirit even came upon seemingly undeserving people to accomplish God's will. Samson, for example, was one of the least deserving people in the Bible for God to work through in a mighty way, and yet He did. The Philistines, the enemies and oppressors of Israel during Samson's day, ambushed the powerful Samson, thinking they had subdued him with ropes. But "the Spirit of the Lord came mightily upon [Samson]; and the ropes that were on his arms became like flax that is burned with fire, and his bonds broke loose from his hands. He found a fresh jawbone of a donkey, reached out his hand and took it, and killed a thousand men with it" (Judges 15:14–15). The Holy Spirit also came upon King Saul of Israel, and King David, and others to empower them to do the will of God.

Whether prophet, priest, or king, shepherd, judge, or soldier, we see the Holy Spirit coming upon people in the Old Testament to empower them to accomplish the will of God.

What Did the Holy Spirit Do in the New Testament?
In the New Testament, the Holy Spirit empowered the ministry of Jesus and His church.

There are a lot of great stories: Cinderella, Sleeping Beauty, Snow White and the Seven Dwarfs. Beauty and the Beast is a great story, though I am referring to the original story, not the Disney animated version familiar to most people. The original story is much better. On a loftier scale, you could add *A Tale of Two Cities*, *Jane Eyre*, and *Les Miserables*. But the greatest story of all time, even for people who do not believe it to be true, is the story of the birth, life, death, and resurrection of Jesus. All the other great stories are shadows and echoes by comparison. The fact that the story of Jesus is true lifts it out of the profound into its own earthshaking category and it cannot be told apart from the Holy Spirit.

Jesus' Birth
In Luke 1:26, the angel Gabriel visited a young Jewish maiden named Mary. Was it in the middle of the night? Was she alone? Was she frightened? He told her she would be having a child. Did he speak to her audibly, or did the thoughts merely enter her mind? Was he visible in any way? Was it a dream or vision? Mary's obvious question was, "How can this be, since I do not know a man?" Gabriel spoke some of the most amazing words ever heard by the human ear: "The Holy Spirit will come upon you, and the power of the Highest will overshadow you; therefore, also, that Holy One who is to be born will be called the Son of God."

What an amazing and touching scene! An unknown Jewish maiden becomes the earthly mother of Jesus of Nazareth by the miraculous conception of the Holy Spirit. From this astonishing beginning, to the bittersweet end, the Holy Spirit was active in and through the life of Jesus.

Jesus' Baptism
When Jesus was baptized, we see the Holy Spirit again, descending on Jesus in the form of a dove (Luke 4:18). This confirmed, along with the voice of God the Father speaking from heaven, the special nature of Jesus' life and empowered Him for ministry. The apostle Peter acknowledges this in Acts 10:38 when

he said, "You know . . . how God anointed Jesus of Nazareth with the Holy Spirit and with power, who went about doing good and healing all who were oppressed by the devil, for God was with Him."

Jesus' Life and Ministry

Immediately after Jesus was baptized, He was led by the Spirit out into the wilderness where He was tempted by Satan (Matthew 4:1–11). John 3:34 says, "For He whom God has sent speaks the words of God; for He gives the Spirit without measure" (NASB). Apparently, God gave the Holy Spirit to Jesus, and that is what enabled Jesus to speak the words of God. Jesus was empowered by the Holy Spirit to do miracles. In Matthew 12:28, we read, "If I (Jesus) cast out demons by the Spirit of God, surely the kingdom of God has come upon you." Jesus' ability to cast out demons was a result of the power of the Holy Spirit within Him.

In summary, we see that Jesus was led by the Spirit, filled with the Spirit, enabled to preach, teach, and exhort by the Spirit, and empowered to do miracles by the Holy Spirit.

Jesus' Death, Burial, and Resurrection

At the end of Jesus' life, the Holy Spirit continued to minister to Him. If Hebrews 9:14 refers to the Holy Spirit, and not Christ's own spirit as some believe, then Jesus offered Himself as a sacrifice through the Holy Spirit: "How much more shall the blood of Christ, who through the eternal Spirit offered Himself without spot to God, cleanse your conscience from dead works to serve the living God?"

Romans 1:4 may refer to the Spirit's involvement in the resurrection of Jesus: "[Jesus] was declared the Son of God with power by the resurrection from the dead, according to the spirit of holiness" (NASB). And finally, Jesus gave commandments to the apostles (and through them to us) by the Holy Spirit: "[Jesus] was taken up, after He through the Holy Spirit had given commandments to the apostles whom He had chosen" (Acts 1:2). So we see, from beginning to end, the Holy Spirit was involved in the life of Jesus of Nazareth.

Revelation

Just as the Holy Spirit revealed God's truth to people in the Old Testament, so He did in the New Testament. He gave people visions and dreams (Acts 10:1–20) and revealed prophecies and

Scripture as He guided the authors of the New Testament (2 Peter 1:21; 3:15–16; 2 Timothy 3:16–17).

The Church

Finally, the Holy Spirit gave birth to the church in the New Testament. In the Old Testament, God chose the nation of Israel to receive His message of salvation and to carry that message to the world (Psalm 67). In the New Testament, God chose the church for that lofty task. It is easy to identify Israel. Israel is all the people who were descendants of Abraham, plus those who converted to Judaism. It is a little harder to identify the church. The church is the totality of all believers in Jesus. When a person becomes a Christian, he automatically becomes a member of the church. It is to the church that God has given the New Testament message of salvation and, it is by the power of the Holy Spirit that the church takes that message to the ends of the earth (Acts 1:8).

What Does the Holy Spirit Do Today?

Today, the Holy Spirit helps Christians know, be, and do what God wants.

After I graduated from seminary, I received a position teaching in a Christian college in Arizona. My wife and I quit our jobs and moved to Arizona in August—not a good time to move. (Someone once said there are three reasons not to live in Arizona: June, July, and August!) School started the first of September. We spent our meager reserves of cash getting moved, paying the deposits on the apartment, utilities, and so forth. And, since we got paid once a month, we were not to receive our first paycheck until the last of September. The bottom line was, we ran out of money. When you run out of money, you also run out of food. We had about two weeks to go before our first paycheck. There was no money in the bank and only about six eggs in the house. We were invited to the academic dean's house for dinner one night, and I must have eaten an unusual amount of food, because somehow the subject turned to how we were making it financially. Since the dean and his wife were asking out of compassion and very directly, we told them. They opened their well-stocked freezer and gave us enough food to last us until our first paycheck. It was slightly humiliating, but deeply appreciated. They helped us when we really needed it.

There have been many times when Margie and I have received help when we really needed it. Sometimes people have helped us load our truck when we were moving. People have let us live with them during periods of transition. Others have sur-

The Holy Spirit is our Helper.

rounded us with love and compassion during times of grave illness. Others have helped us capitalize on opportunities by putting in a good word for us. Friends have come close to us when we were lonely. When we look back over our lives, we see an endless stream of people who helped us overcome difficulties or just made life easier.

You are doing something godly when you help others, because that is the primary ministry of God the Holy Spirit to us—to help us. Five times in the Gospel of John the Holy Spirit is called our Helper. If we were to summarize what the Holy Spirit does today, we would say that He helps those who are Christians.

When we are down, He helps us up. When we need a shove, He gets us moving in the right direction. When we need wisdom, He opens our mind to God's word. He helps us witness to Jesus both by opening the door of opportunity and by giving us the words to share. The Holy Spirit helps believers in many ways, as the rest of the book will demonstrate.

What Will the Holy Spirit Do in the Future?

In the future, the Holy Spirit will help bring history to an end and usher in eternity.

We don't know as much about the future as we wish we did. We would like to know how things are going to unfold for us personally, when the end of the world will come, and what life will be like after that. We also do not know as much about the ministry of the Holy Spirit in the future as we wish we did. Most of what is said about the Spirit's ministry in the future is veiled in mystery, and there are usually at least two responsible opinions as to what the Scripture means in these instances.

Some believe that 2 Thessalonians 2:7 teaches that there will be a day when the Holy Spirit, who restrains sin in the world, will be removed from the earth as a pervasive presence restraining sin, and that a conflagration of sin will erupt like an unattended forest fire. Others believe that when Joel 2 was quoted in Acts

2:17–21 it was not a complete fulfillment of Joel's prophecy, so the prophecy will be finally fulfilled at some time in the future. If that is the case, the Spirit will be involved in some pretty dramatic events in the future, such as the sun turning to darkness and the moon turning to blood, and visions and dreams being rather widespread.

Also, in comparing Zechariah 4:1–6 with Revelation 11:3–4, we see the Holy Spirit being involved in some rather apocalyptic events at some time in the future. How literally these events are to be interpreted and when they might happen is not a matter of complete agreement in the Christian community, so the Spirit's role here is a matter of educated speculation. But whatever these passages mean, we see the Spirit involved and His power revealed to an awesome extent.

Conclusion

To conclude this overview chapter, I want to focus on the whole subject of helping others. There is an old poem which reads,

Let me live in my house by the side of the road
  Where the race of men go by—
They are good, they are bad, they are weak, they are strong.
  Wise, foolish—so am I.
Then why should I sit in the scorner's seat
  Or hurl the cynic's ban?
Let me live in my house by the side of the road
  And be a friend to man.
(Sam Walter Foss, "The House by the Side of the Road," quoted by William Bennett, *The Book of Virtues* 305–306.)

It sounds foreign to us today. It is so risky to help people. If you pick up a hitchhiker, he may rob you and steal your car. If you open your door to a stranger on a stormy night, he may assault you. If you give money to someone who seems to need it, he may have lied to you and spend the money on drugs or alcohol.

Today, therefore, we might write,

Let me live in my house on the cul-de-sac
  where no one ever drives by.

Men are bad, they are weak, they will lie and will steal.
    Be a victim? No, not I.
Let them ply their wicked trade of life
    On less suspecting souls.
Let me live in my house on the cul-de-sac
    Where trouble never tolls.

It is certainly true that life is more complicated than it used to be. It is harder to help people than it used to be, but that doesn't mean we should stop trying. Certainly it may be unwise to put ourselves or our families in danger, but there are a thousand "safe" ways we can help people if we will.

One day as my wife and I were coming home from church, we saw a car stranded on the highway. I pulled over and walked up to the driver's window, which had a white handkerchief flying from it. An obviously frightened lady rolled the window down about half an inch and said, "My car has quit running. Could you call the police for me?" I stood away from the car, so as not to intimidate her unnecessarily. I said, "Ma'am, I'll be at my home in five minutes and will call the police from there. There should be someone here in ten or fifteen minutes. Don't worry. I won't fail to get someone here to help you." We met a police car on the way home, and he was at her car within five minutes.

It's a small thing, but thirty-five years ago, when I was a teenager, that lady would have gotten out of her car, and we would have talked about what was wrong with the doggone thing. I might even have taken her someplace so she didn't have to wait in the car. Not today. But we still can help.

People still need our help.

Churches often get calls from people needing money or help of some kind, and many times you don't know if the calls are legitimate. I had to develop a policy of almost never giving anyone money, because we discovered that panhandlers who wanted the money for alcohol soon learned who the "soft touches" were. It was like getting your name on some bad mailing list. You soon had more sob stories than you knew how to handle. We would buy people groceries, or pay their rent or electric bill, but almost never give them money.

I'll never forget one man calling me three different times over a six-month period. He had a rich, distinctive voice, and he apparently didn't keep good records of whom he had tried to fleece, because each time, in a plaintive, wavering voice that would bring tears to the eyes of Attila the Hun, he would tell me of how his wife's mother had just died, and they needed only $100 more to fly back to Ohio for the funeral. The first time, I offered to meet with him to go buy the tickets together, but there was a reason why that wouldn't work. He said he'd call me back, but never did. The second time was like an instant replay, but I wasn't sure it was the same person, though it seemed like quite a coincidence. The third time, I said, "Sir, you've told me this story three times. How many times are they going to bury your mother-in-law?" I never got another call from him.

There were times when the appeals for help were obviously legitimate and times when they obviously weren't. But there were times when you just didn't know. In those times, as a church, we decided God would rather have us waste some of His money on people who didn't deserve it than fail to give it to someone who really needed it.

Yes, it is hard to help people these days. But if we have a heart that lives "by the side of the road" instead of on the cul-de-sac, we will find ways to help that are safe and appropriate. And when you help others, you are imitating what God does for us every day.

Speed Bump!
Slow down to be sure you've gotten the main points of this chapter.

Question
Answer

Q1. What did the Holy Spirit do in the Old Testament?

A1. In the Old Testament, the Holy Spirit *helped* in creation, revealed truth to people, and empowered people to do God's will.

Q2. What did the Holy Spirit do in the New Testament?

A2. In the New Testament, the Holy Spirit *empowered* the ministry of Jesus and His church.

Q3. What does the Holy Spirit do today?

A3. Today, the Holy Spirit *helps* Christians know, be, and do what God wants.

Q4. What will the Holy Spirit do in the future?

A4. In the future, the Holy Spirit will *help* bring history to an end and usher in eternity.

Fill in the Blank

Question
Answer

Q1. What did the Holy Spirit do in the Old Testament?

A1. In the Old Testament, the Holy Spirit _____ in creation, revealed truth to people, and empowered people to do God's will.

Q2. What did the Holy Spirit do in the New Testament?

A2. In the New Testament, the Holy Spirit _____ the ministry of Jesus and His church.

Q3. What does the Holy Spirit do today?

A3. Today, the Holy Spirit _____ Christians know, be, and do what God wants.

Q4. What will the Holy Spirit do in the future?

A4. In the future, the Holy Spirit will _____ bring history to an end and usher in eternity.

For Further Thought and Discussion

1. What observations can you make about the differences between the ministry of the Holy Spirit in the Old Testament and the New Testament?

2. What new observations did you learn about the relationship of the Holy Spirit to Jesus? How would you describe His ministry to Jesus?

3. Often, we are not aware of the Holy Spirit's helping ministry to us, but seeing that the primary role of the Holy Spirit is to "help" Christians, can you recall a time when you feel confident the Holy Spirit helped you in some obvious way?

4. Mentally, do you live in a house closer to the side of the road or a house closer to the cul-de-sac? Why? What is one positive change you might need to make regarding your mind-set?

What If I Don't Believe?

1. Concerning His work in creation, I will have a deficient view of the cooperative ministries of the Father, Son, and Holy Spirit, and of the full deity of the Holy Spirit.

2. Concerning His ministry to Jesus, I will have a low view of the sacrificial commitment the members of the Godhead have to one another.

3. Concerning His ministry to believers, I will have an incomplete view of His role in our lives.

4. Concerning the future, I will not understand that the Holy Spirit continues to be God in the future as well as the present and past.

For Further Study

1. Scripture
Several passages speak to the role of the Holy Spirit. They include:

- Genesis 1
- Judges 15:14–15
- 2 Samuel 23:1–2
- Psalm 67
- Matthew 4:1–11
- Luke 1:35
- Luke 4:18
- Acts 2:17–21
- Acts 10:38
- Romans 1:4

2. Books
Several other books are very helpful in studying this subject. They are listed below in general order of difficulty. If I could read only one of these, I would read the first one:

Flying Closer to the Flame, Charles Swindoll
A Survey of Bible Doctrine, Charles Ryrie
Essential Truths of the Christian Faith, R. C. Sproul
Concise Theology, James I. Packer

*Through his death on the cross Jesus Christ
not only readjusts a man in conscience and
heart to God, he does something grander; he
imparts to him the power to do all God wants,
he presences him with divinity, the Holy
Spirit, so that he is garrisoned from within,
and enabled to live without blame before
God.*
■ Oswald Chambers (1874–1917)

What Is the Role of the Holy Spirit in My Salvation?

I grew up in a moral home. I never heard my mother or father swear, tell an off-color joke, act unkindly toward others, or say unkind things about others. They were rock-solid moral people, and we were a moral family. In high school, I hung around with people who were pretty moral, and I never got into trouble or did anything bad. I was pretty energetic and talkative and nearly drove a few teachers nuts, but it was not malicious, just exasperating. I didn't drink, use drugs, use vulgar language, take advantage of girls, steal, vandalize, or anything else like that. I was not, however, a Christian.

When I went to college, I left my family and friends behind and entered a totally different world, where drinking, drugs, vulgar language, sexual freedom, cheating, and stealing were cherished values. Because I was not a Christian, and had nothing stronger than my family heritage and former peer group to keep me straight, I began to do things that even I didn't agree with. Instead of being a clean-cut athlete hanging around with other clean-cut athletes, I began playing cards in the student union all day (when I should have been in class), and playing drums in a rock band all night. And (to say it the kindest way possible) not everyone I hung around with was clean-cut. Come to think of it, no one was. I never studied except the night before a test, when I would stay up all night cramming, then go in and do my best. My best was not very good. I would try to get other people to write my papers for me. I wasn't a very good judge of ability, because I didn't get very good grades with their papers. My grade point average began to suffer seriously.

As someone has said, "If you don't stand for something, you'll fall for anything." I fell for anything. I adopted the lifestyle of those around me and went the way of the world. I admit that I had a lot of fun from time to time. But whenever the fun was over, there was an aching void, a sense of meaningless and purposelessness. In addition, my self-esteem collapsed. *Why did I do those things?* I wondered. I wanted to live a better life, but I seemed powerless to withstand the flow of the life I was in. Finally, I fell into such deep guilt and remorse than I underwent a temporary personality change. I became brooding, sullen, and morose. I would "fly off the handle" at the least provocation. I was miserable.

In this chapter we learn . . .

Five key roles the Holy Spirit plays in our salvation:

1. Conviction: causing us to recognize our sin and prompting us to turn from it.
2. Regeneration: causing us to be born again, spiritually, resulting in eternal life.
3. Indwelling: coming to live in the body of each Christian.
4. Baptism: incorporating the Christian into the body of Christ.
5. Sealing: marking us as God's own possession and guaranteeing our salvation.

My foolish and sinful lifestyle, along with a growing apprehension about death, brought me to such despair that I was ready to listen when someone told me that Christ could save me, give me eternal life in heaven as well as a new life on earth—the life I wanted. That is what led me to the conversation with Jake Berger that I mentioned in the previous chapter. Guilt and remorse over my sin, plus a desire to have the strength to live a better life, were major forces in persuading me to become a Christian, which I did the summer after my first dissipated year in a state university.

What I didn't realize then, but I know now, is that I was experiencing the convicting ministry of the Holy Spirit. The deep remorse, the sense of meaninglessness, the longing for something better were all part of His ministry in bringing me to salvation. This was not a natural process. Plenty of people live much worse lives than I did and feel not a twinge of conscience. I know. Many of them were my friends. No, when someone turns to Christ, it is not a work of man; it is a work of God. Of course, If you had asked me at the time, I would not have thought that God had anything to do with it. But looking back, and comparing my experience with the truth of Scripture, it is clear that God was at work.

This is the reason it is so important for Christian or non-Christian alike to respond whenever they feel drawn to God and away from sin. You cannot make that move unless God is working in your heart. At other times in my life I knew I should have cleaned up my act, but I wasn't really interested. It didn't really bother me all that much. Why? God wasn't working. A person must have the ministry of the Holy

---

Why I need to know the role of the Holy Spirit in my salvation:

1. I need to understand that I cannot come to Christ except as He is working in my life. The same is true about others to whom I may be ministering.
2. If I don't understand this, it might put me on a guilt trip, thinking that if I had done more, someone else might have become a Christian. If I don't understand that I am merely a conveyer of information—that salvation is between a person and God—I may take up a burden that is simply too great for me to carry.
3. If I don't understand the Holy Spirit's role in my salvation, I will not appreciate completely what He has done for me, and it will limit my joy and my capacity to worship God.

Spirit to become a Christian. He cannot make that decision unaided, and that is the focus of this chapter. We must understand the work of the Holy Spirit in our salvation, or else (1) we may not come to salvation, and (2) if we do, we will not have a great enough appreciation for the work of God that was done, so, (3) we will not have sufficient gratitude and capacity for worship and praise.

The Holy Spirit does many things to bring us to salvation. We will look at five primary ones: conviction, regeneration, indwelling, baptism, and sealing.

What Is Conviction?

Conviction is the ministry of the Holy Spirit in which He causes us to recognize our sin and prompts us to turn from it.

Central Passage: John 16:8, *When He* [the Holy Spirit] *has come, He will convict the world of sin, and of righteousness, and of judgment.*

Conviction was what I experienced during my moral collapse in my first year in college—the gut-wrenching realization that I was trapped in a lifestyle that I didn't want but didn't have the strength to pull myself out of. I understood very well where the phrase "guilty as sin" came from. I felt guilty as sin, because I was. I believed I was sinning and ought to stop. That is the beginning point for salvation. Even if someone understands all about salvation, he will make no attempt to receive it unless he first comes to recognize that he is a sinner and wants to do something about it. When you are discussing salvation with someone and he has no conviction of sin, no sense of his need for Christ, you will get nowhere. There were times in my life when people talked to me about salvation, and I told them to mind their own business. I had no conviction of sin. I had no sense of separation from God and a need to be reconciled to Him.

In 2 Corinthians 4:3–4, we read, "If our gospel is veiled, it is veiled to those who are perishing, whose minds the god of this age [Satan] has blinded, who do not believe, lest the light of the gospel of the glory of Christ, who is the image of God, should shine on them." As long as someone is blinded by Satan, he will feel no conviction of sin. That is why, when we talk or preach or write to others about Christ, our first line of offense is prayer. Our clever arguments will never win anyone to Christ. Our

Without the Spirit, our witness gets nowhere.

powers of persuasion, our magnetic personality, our depth of relationship are all as powerless as a floodlight on a forest fire to convince anyone of a need for Christ. Only if the person is convicted of sin, recognizes that sin has separated him from God, and desires to be reconciled to God will that one accept the gospel of Christ.

As I said, no one can bring another person to Christ. Only God can bring someone to Christ, and conviction of sin is the first step. This is what was behind Jesus' statement in John 6:44, "No one can come to Me unless the Father who sent Me draws him; and I will raise him up at the last day." The Father draws us through the Holy Spirit.

Therefore, in sharing our faith we must recognize that our task is to pray and rely on God entirely for His work in the life of the individual with whom we are dealing. We are responsible to share Christ with others, but we cannot determine whether or not that person will come to Christ. That is between the person and Christ.

I have seen people beat themselves up emotionally, saying, "Why didn't I do thus and such, or why didn't I say this or that? If only I had, Joe or Sally would have come to Christ."

Maybe they would have and maybe they wouldn't. There are those who have come to Christ on the prompting of the slightest off-the-cuff remark, and there are those who have been raised in godly Christian homes, hearing the truth and seeing it lived all their lives, who never come to Christ. Salvation is a work of God, not a work of man. Proclamation is our work. We give the Good News and we pray. God does everything else.

What Is Regeneration?

Regeneration is the ministry of the Holy Spirit in which He causes us to be born again, spiritually, resulting in eternal life.

Central Passage: Titus 3:5 (NASB), *He saved us, not on the basis of deeds which we have done in righteousness, but according to His mercy, by the washing of regeneration and renewing by the Holy Spirit.*

Phoenix was the Greek name for the mythological bird that was sacred to the sun-god in ancient Egypt. An eaglelike bird with red and gold plumage (as Herodotus described it), the phoenix lived in Arabia and had a five hundred-year life span. At the end of that period the bird built its own funeral pyre, on which it was consumed to ashes. Out of the ashes a new phoenix arose. The cycle was repeated every five hundred years.

In a sense, that is what happens to the Christian. Mankind has self-destructed, burning himself to ashes on his own funeral pyre of sin. "But God, who is rich in mercy, because of His great love with which He loved us, even when we were dead in trespasses, made us alive together with Christ" (Ephesians 2:4–5). Out of the ashes, we rise to new life in Christ. The dramatic story of the phoenix became popular with some medieval Christian writers as a symbol of death and resurrection.

"We were dead in our trespasses and sins," Paul wrote. In what sense were we dead? Obviously we were not dead physically. We were dead spiritually, which means separated from

God. It is like a husband and wife who no longer love each other. Hostility and rejection lie at the core of their relationship. They do not talk to each other. They no longer live in the same house. Their relationship, we say, is dead. It means more than that to be dead in our trespasses and sins before God, but at least that example gives us a glimpse of the meaning. It does not mean that we have ceased living, spiritually. It means we are separated, cut off, alienated from God.

Eternal life follows death to sin.

Our spirit has been contaminated with sin, and God cannot tolerate the presence of sin. Therefore, apart from His amazing love for us, He cannot tolerate us. There is only one hope. Our old self, contaminated with sin, must die. That is what Paul meant when he said, "I have been crucified with Christ" (Galatians 2:20). Spiritually, in a way we do not fully understand, we are placed in Christ, and the crucifixion that He experienced, we experience. The death that He died, we die. That gets rid of the sin. Then, by the ministry of the Holy Spirit, we are born again, this time, to new life. This time, we are without sin in our inner man (Romans 7:15—8:1).

We still sin, but somehow, again in ways that I am not sure we fully understand, the sin is not attributed to our spirit, our inner man; it is assigned to our flesh. There is nothing else that needs to happen to our spirit before it can go to heaven. Paul wrote in Ephesians 4:24 (NASB), "Put on the new self which, in the likeness of God has been created in righteousness and holiness of the truth." What an astonishing statement. Our new self, after we have been born again, is in the likeness of God, in righteousness and holiness.

New birth makes us righteous before God.

Of course, we all know that we sin, but Paul steadfastly refuses to attribute the sin to the new self. He goes out of his way to place it in what he calls "the flesh" (NASB). "If I am doing the very thing I do not wish, I am no longer the one doing it, but sin which dwells in me" (Romans 7:20 NASB).

He completes this thought in Romans 8:23: "We ourselves groan within ourselves, eagerly waiting for the adoption, the redemption of our body." His point here is that our complete redemption will not occur until we die and get a new body, uncontaminated by sin. We could say that we are redeemed in stages. One stage is our spiritual redemption when we are born again.

Another stage is our progressive spiritual growth while on earth. A third stage is our physical redemption, when we receive new bodies, either when we die or when Jesus comes again, whichever comes first.

Regeneration is that act of the Holy Spirit by which He causes us to be born again, spiritually, at the moment we place our faith in Christ.

With this as background, read the condensed account from John 3 where Jesus talks to Nicodemus, a religious leader of the Jews, about his need to be born again, and see if it doesn't make sense to you:

> Now there was a man of the Pharisees, named Nicodemus, a ruler of the Jews; this man came to Him by night, and said to Him, "Rabbi, we know that You have come from God as a teacher; for no one can do these signs that You do unless God is with him." Jesus answered and said to him, "Truly, truly, I say to you, unless one is born again, he cannot see the kingdom of God." Nicodemus said to Him, "How can a man be born when he is old? He cannot enter a second time into his mother's womb and be born, can he?" Jesus answered, "Truly, truly, I say to you, unless one is born of . . . the Spirit, he cannot enter into the kingdom of God. . . . Do not marvel that I said to you, 'You must be born again.' . . . As Moses lifted up the serpent in the wilderness, even so must the Son of Man be lifted up, that whoever believes may in Him have eternal life. For God so loved the world, that He gave His only begotten Son, that whoever believes in Him should not perish, but have eternal life. (NASB)

One of the ministries that the Holy Spirit has in our salvation is causing us to be born again, spiritually, resulting in eternal life.

What Is Indwelling?

Indwelling is the ministry of the Holy Spirit coming to live in the body of each Christian.

Central Passage: 1 Corinthians 6:19–20, *Do you not know that your body is the temple of the Holy Spirit who is in you, whom you have from God, and you are not your own? For you were bought at a price; therefore glorify God in your body.*

Misunderstanding the concept of "indwelling" was where I got into trouble the night I became a Christian. As I said, I had the idea that there was a Max-shaped spirit sitting beside me that I had to get to merge with my shape, like focusing a camera or a pair of binoculars. The concept of indwelling is such a mystery that probably none of us understands specifically what happens in the process. But indwelt we are if we give our lives over to following Christ. The Scripture makes it clear that the Holy Spirit is in us, and based on that fact, we should glorify God in our bodies.

Every believer is permanently indwelt. The Holy Spirit does not move in and move out like an unstable tenant. Nor does He move in and out depending on whether he likes the condition of the "temple" He is in. Indwelling is permanent. Once He comes to take up residence in you, He stays forever. Jesus made that plain when he

Indwelling is once and for always.

said, "I will pray the Father, and He will give you another Helper, that He may abide with you forever—the Spirit of truth, whom the world cannot receive, because it neither sees Him nor knows Him; but you know Him, for He dwells with you and will be in you" (John 14:16–17).

We sometimes fear that if we sin the Holy Spirit will leave us. While there are plenty of things to dread if we willfully and flagrantly persist in sin (Hebrews 12:5–11), losing the Holy Spirit is not one of them. As we just saw, Jesus sent the Helper "that He may abide with you forever."

If anyone was going to lose the Holy Spirit, it would have been some of the Christians in the ancient church in Corinth. One church member was committing adultery with his stepmother (1 Corinthians 5:5)! Others were suing the socks off each other (1 Corinthians 6)! Others apparently were visiting prostitutes (1 Corinthians 6:15). Paul says of them, "You are still not spiritual, because there is jealousy and quarreling among you, and this shows that you are not spiritual. You are acting like people of the world" (1 Corinthians 3:3, New Century Version). And so they were—somewhat like the church in America! Yet, in spite of this, Paul tells these people that the indwelling of the Spirit is permanent. It is precisely because the Holy Spirit is indwelling them that Paul urges them not to defile their bodies with sexual immorality (Romans 6:18–20).

There are two ways a Christian can know that he is indwelt

by the Holy Spirit. First, simply take the Scripture at face value. If you have believed in and received Christ as your personal savior, you have the Spirit. In fact, Romans 8:9 makes it clear that if you don't have the Spirit you are not saved, while if you do have the Spirit, you are. The second way is to look for the evidence of His work in your life. When I became a Christian, I was not sure I was, because I couldn't keep the Holy Spirit's spiritual outline in focus with my physical outline. But the next day, I went to work at my summer construction job, and it really bothered me that everyone was swearing. No matter that the day before I was leading the uncouth chorus, today I wanted everybody to shut up. *Why did they have to take Jesus' name in vain?* I wondered. I also quit drinking, smoking, and hanging out with the wrong kind of people. On the other side of things, I found myself reading my Bible, especially the Gospel of John, over and over again. I started going to church, and developed a desire to talk to other Christians about spiritual things. A desire to be more loving, less prideful, and more patient sprang up deep within me. Not everyone's experience will be the same as mine, but "change" is a sign of the indwelling Spirit of God.

Because the Spirit indwells us, we are never alone. Prisoners in concentration camps or prisoner of war camps testify that the presence of God kept them going during the grueling hours, days, and even years of solitude, because they knew they were not really alone.

What Is Baptism?

Baptism of the Holy Spirit is the ministry of the Spirit incorporating the Christian into the body of Christ.

Central Passage: Romans 6:3–5 (NASB), *Or do you not know that all of us who have been baptized into Christ Jesus have been baptized into His death? Therefore we have been buried with Him through baptism into death, in order that as Christ was raised from the dead through the glory of the Father, so we too might walk in newness of life. For if we have become united with Him in the likeness of His death, certainly we shall be also in the likeness of His resurrection.*

Christians agree widely concerning the Holy Spirit's work in our salvation, and that body of agreement provides a common perspective on much of the Christian life. The definition and purpose of the baptism of the Holy Spirit, however, is one of the areas that is widely debated. While we look at varying perspectives in this section, we emphasize that, while there may be differences of understanding on this issue among Christians, there is fundamental agreement on the basics of the Christian faith that we share, and we therefore survey the differences with a spirit of mutual respect.

The Classic Evangelical View

The mainstream evangelical position, which reflects my own view, understands baptism of the Holy Spirit to be that work of the Holy Spirit in which He places each believer into the body of Christ at the moment of conversion. First Corinthians 12:13 says, "For by one Spirit we were all baptized into one body—whether Jews or Greeks, whether slaves or free—and have all been made to drink into one Spirit."

From the central passage in Romans 6, from Acts 1:4–5 and from this Corinthian passage, evangelicals draw several observations:

1. All believers are baptized by the Spirit.
2. Spirit baptism happens at the moment of conversion.
3. Apparently each believer is baptized only once.
4. It makes all believers members of the body of Christ.

The Body of Christ: The body of Christ is a figure of speech, meaning "the totality of all believers in Jesus." It is the totality of all Christians who have ever lived, past, present, and future. It is synonymous in the Bible with the "Church." This "Universal Church" is the same as the body of Christ. Local churches are local, visible, organized groups of people who may or may not be members of the Universal Church, the body of Christ. If a person is not a Christian, he may attend a local church, even be a member of the local church. But because he is not a Christian, he is not a member of the Universal Church, the Body of Christ. You may have heard the old saying that going to local church doesn't make a person a Christian any more than going to a barn makes someone a cow, or going to a garage makes someone a car. That is the point here.

Baptize: To baptize means, primarily, "to dip." It is used in the Bible of people taking baths, of dying a garment, or of drawing water by dipping a cup into the water.

To be baptized by the Holy Spirit, according to this perspective, means to be placed, or incorporated spiritually into the body of Christ. It is as if the body of Christ were an ocean of people, and we, as individuals, are placed into it. "We have been buried with Him through *baptism* into death," Paul writes in Romans 6:3 (NASB, italics added). Verse 5 goes on to mention that "if we have become *united* with Him in the likeness of His death, certainly we shall be also in the likeness of His resurrection (NASB, italics added)." The inference can be drawn, then, that being baptized into Christ means "being united with Him," as well as with all other believers in the body of Christ.

Some evangelicals apply the term baptism to one's first experience of being filled with the Spirit. However, many evangelicals understand that while speaking in tongues and other miraculous events occurred in the New Testament, they were not a manifestation of the baptism of the Holy Spirit, but rather a result of the miraculous filling of the Holy Spirit (Acts 2:4). The filling of the Holy Spirit will be discussed in a later chapter. The baptism of the Spirit, as we said, simply places one into the spiritual body of Christ.

Billy Graham articulated this view of Spirit baptism in his book, *The Holy Spirit*, when he wrote:

Many years ago when I was attending a small Bible school in Florida, I visited what was called a "brush arbor revival meeting." The speaker was an old fashioned Southern revival preacher. The little place seated about two hundred people and was filled. The speaker made up in thunder what he lacked in logic, and the people loved it.

"Have you been baptized with the Holy Spirit?"

Apparently he knew a great many in the audience because he would point to someone and ask, "Brother, have you been baptized with the Spirit?" And the man would answer, "Yes, bless God."

"Young man," he said, spotting me, "have you been baptized with the Holy Spirit?" "Yes, sir," I replied.

"When were you baptized with the Holy Spirit?" he asked. He had not questioned the others on this.

"The moment I received Jesus Christ as my Savior," I replied.

He looked at me with a puzzled expression, but before going to the next person he said, "That couldn't be."

But it could! It was.

I do not doubt the sincerity of this preacher. However, in my own study of the Scriptures through the years I have become convinced that there is only one baptism with the Holy Spirit in the life of every believer, and that takes place at the moment of conversion (89–90).

The Pentecostal/Charismatic View

Perhaps Graham had attended a Pentecostal revival. In the Pentecostal and charismatic view, "baptism in the Holy Spirit" differs from the mainstream evangelical view both in its definition and its purpose. In this view, Jesus baptizes already converted believers with the Holy Spirit in order to empower them to live and minister as Jesus did.

They believe this for two key reasons: the example of Jesus and the example of the early church in Acts. Regarding Jesus, when He was baptized by John the Baptist, the Holy Spirit descended upon Him, and He was described as "being filled with the Holy Spirit" when He entered His forty days of temptation (Luke 3:22; 4:1). After His temptation, Jesus entered public ministry "in the power of the Spirit" and with the Spirit's anointing (Luke 4:14, 18–19).

This tradition emphasizes that Jesus is to be seen not only as unique, but also as an example to be followed. As God, as Messiah, as Savior, as the Son of God, Jesus is unique and unrepeatable. But as one whose ministry is empowered by the Holy Spirit, Jesus is a prototype for all believers who may and can be similarly empowered by the Holy Spirit to continue Jesus' earthly ministry now that He is gone.

The book of Acts begins by strongly connecting the ministry of Jesus while He was on earth with His ongoing ministry through the early church (Acts 1:1). While the Gospel of Luke, the companion to Acts, recorded what "Jesus began to do and teach," Acts records what Jesus continued to do through the divine power of the Holy Spirit and Jesus' followers. Just as Jesus Himself was empowered by the Holy Spirit, so believers are to be also. The "Promise of the Father" is given when Jesus baptizes believers with (or by or in) the Holy Spirit, Who empowers believers to witness effectively to Jesus throughout the world (Acts 1:4–8).

The Pentecostal/charismatic view of Spirit baptism links Jesus' ministry with the similar experiences of his followers in the book of Acts when the Spirit came upon them (2:1–4; 4:31; 8:14–17; 11:12–17; 19:1–6). Baptism in the Holy Spirit is seen to be distinct from conversion (although nothing in principle prevents Spirit baptism at conversion) and distinct from the purpose of incorporating a believer into Christ's body. Spirit baptism instead introduces the Christian to the fullness of the Christian life that God intended. It also empowers the believer for effective ministry, complete with the same kinds of supernatural works that characterize His ministry.

Drawing upon the examples in the book of Acts of the Spirit's coming upon and filling believers, Pentecostals and charismatics understand that when believers are baptized in the Spirit, they know it: The coming of the Spirit is experienced, as the various descriptions of Acts indicate, usually including speaking in tongues. Some Pentecostals and charismatics do not insist that Spirit baptism is always accompanied by speaking in tongues, but do maintain that some sort of Spirit-inspired speech signifies the Spirit's coming and giving the power to witness to Christ effectively.

Traditional Wesleyan teaching also emphasizes that the baptism of the Holy Spirit is distinct from conversion and leads to fullness of Christian life and effective service. Generally, however, Wesleyan believers do not embrace other Pentecostal and charismatic practices, such as speaking in tongues.

While the Pentecostal/charismatic tradition sees the baptism of the Holy Spirit as distinct from conversion (unlike the classic evangelical view that sees it as part of and simultaneous with conversion), it is seen as part of an essential process, the whole of which includes "conversion + water baptism + Spirit baptism" (see Acts 2:38). That is, God wants each Christian to experience conversion, water baptism, and Spirit baptism as entry into the fullness of Christian life and ministry.

Conversion is essential, of course, because that is the moment at which a person becomes a Christian. *Water baptism* is important because it is commanded by our Lord (Matthew 28:19–20). *Spirit baptism* is important because it is essential to empower the Christian for fullness of the Christian life and full effectiveness in ministry.

Other issues related closely to the Pentecostal/charismatic tradition's understanding of the Holy Spirit baptism, such as the role of signs and wonders and spiritual gifts in contemporary biblical Christianity, will be addressed elsewhere in the book.

Summary

All evangelical Christians, including those in the Pentecostal/charismatic tradition who differ on their understanding of "baptism of the Holy Spirit," agree that the Holy Spirit incorporates all believers into the body of Christ at the point of their conversion and new birth. All evangelical Christians also believe that miraculous things happened in the book of Acts surrounding the fillings and baptisms of the Holy Spirit. The two primary differences in understanding between the two traditions include the definition of Spirit baptism (and whether or not the miraculous events in Acts were a result of that baptism or of a special Spirit filling) and whether the miracles accompanying the lives of Jesus and His disciples are intended to be duplicated in the ministry of the church in all times.

What Is Sealing?

Sealing of the Holy Spirit is the ministry of the Spirit marking us as God's own possession and guaranteeing our salvation.

Central Passage: Ephesians 1:13–14 (NASB), *In* [Christ], *you also, after listening to the message of truth, the gospel of your salvation—having also believed, you were sealed in Him with the Holy Spirit of promise, who is given as a pledge of our inheritance.*

The sealing of the Holy Spirit marks us as God's own possession. The Holy Spirit within us is that mark. One of the best days of my life came when I was invited to participate with a rancher in branding the yearling calves. We rode out onto the range and drove the cattle with new calves to a holding pen. There we caught each calf and burned a brand into its hip. The brand is unique, registered to that rancher. No other rancher can have the same brand. The brand says, "This calf belongs to John Q. Rancher," and no one can dispute it. The Holy Spirit is God's brand on us.

Sealing signifies ownership and authority.

Not only does the seal signify ownership, it also signifies authority. One of my favorite stories picturing the power and significance of a seal is that of an emissary that Alexander the Great once sent to Egypt. This representative of the most powerful man on earth at the time traveled to Egypt without weapons or military escort. He carried only the seal of Alexander, possibly a signet ring bearing Alexander's official seal.

The emissary met with the king of Egypt, who stood with his army behind him, and communicated to him that Alexander wanted him to cease hostilities against Alexander's interests. The king of Egypt, wishing to save face, said that he would consider Alexander's request and let him know later what his response would be.

At that, the emissary drew a circle in the dirt around the king of Egypt and said, "Do not leave the circle without informing me of your response."

Think of that! The king of Egypt was standing there in full military array, with his army instantly ready to obey his commands. The emissary was unarmed. Yet the king dared not harm or defy the emissary without defying Alexander. Whatever he did to the emissary, he did to Alexander. Realizing that he was facing, by extension, Alexander himself, after a long, tense moment he said, "Tell Alexander he has his request," and stepped out of the circle.

That is the power of a seal. It carries the full weight of the one who owns it. We have God's seal, the Holy Spirit, which carries the full weight of God the Father behind it (2 Corinthians 1:22). The seal signifies that we are God's possession, that we have God's authority behind us, and it guarantees our security.

This seal, Paul says in Ephesians 1:13–14, is also a pledge, a down payment. The presence of the Holy Spirit indwelling us guarantees the final purchase price when our bodies are redeemed in heaven.

The trucking industry provides another interesting illustration of the sealing of the Spirit. For certain types of loads, when a truck is fully loaded and ready for its run, a plastic seal is put around the lock on the door. Breaking this seal before the truck reaches its destination will mean the loss of one's job. This is similar to the sealing of the Spirit. The seal of the Spirit cannot be broken before the Christian reaches his heavenly destination. It is our guarantee of reaching the destination God intends for us.

Conclusion

All these ministries of the Holy Spirit to us are simultaneous at the moment of salvation. While the conviction process may be long and drawn-out previous to salvation, we are not saved without it. It is still present at the moment of salvation, convincing us to repent, to turn from our previous attitudes about Christ, and to accept Him as our personal savior. Regeneration, indwelling, baptism, and sealing all occur the moment we say "yes" to the invitation of Christ.

Speed Bump!

Slow down to be sure you've gotten the main points of this chapter.

Question
Answer

Q1. What is conviction?

A1. Conviction is the ministry of the Holy Spirit in which He causes us to recognize our *sin* and prompts us to turn from it.

Q2. What is regeneration?

A2. Regeneration is the ministry of the Holy Spirit in which He causes us to be born again, spiritually, resulting in eternal life.

Q3. What is indwelling?

A3. Indwelling is the ministry of the Holy Spirit coming to *live* in the body of each Christian.

Q4. What is baptism?

A4. Baptism of the Holy Spirit is the ministry of the Spirit *incorporating* the Christian into the body of Christ.

Q5. What is sealing?

A5. Sealing of the Holy Spirit is the ministry of the Spirit *marking* us as God's own possession and guaranteeing our salvation.

Fill in the Blank

Question
Answer

Q1. What is conviction?

A1. Conviction is the ministry of the Holy Spirit in which He causes us to recognize our _____ and prompts us to turn from it.

Q2. What is regeneration?

A2. Regeneration is the ministry of the Holy Spirit in which He causes us
to be _____ _____, spiritually, resulting in eternal
life.

Q3. What is indwelling?

A3. Indwelling is the ministry of the Holy Spirit coming to _____
in the body of each Christian.

Q4. What is baptism?

A4. Baptism of the Holy Spirit is the ministry of the Spirit _____
the Christian into the body of Christ.

Q5. What is sealing?

A5. Sealing of the Holy Spirit is the ministry of the Spirit _____ us
as God's own possession and guaranteeing our salvation.

For Further Thought and Discussion

1. Regeneration, indwelling, baptism, and sealing may occur without a
great emotional experience. We must accept these ministries by faith as
we read of them in the Scripture. We may have emotional consequences,
such as relief or joy as a result of our salvation. What response do you
have to the knowledge of the Holy Spirit's role in your salvation? Can
you describe it in a word, or would it take a paragraph?

2. In your own experience, how has the Holy Spirit convicted you of your
sin and need for salvation? Has it been a more emotional matter (guilt,
remorse, longing), or a more intellectual matter (seeing the truth of
Scripture, seeing the logic, grasping the significance of Christ's death,
burial, and resurrection)? Describe.

3. How do you think this understanding of the Holy Spirit's work in
salvation will affect your relationship with Him? How do you think it
will affect your worship? How do you think it will affect your prayer?

What If I Don't Believe?

1. I may reject the convicting ministry of the Holy Spirit as mere twinges
of human conscience and miss the work God is wanting to do in my
life.

2. Continual rejection of the Holy Spirit's convicting work will result in a hardening of my conscience. He will be less and less able to move me in His direction.

3. I will have a diminished capacity to appreciate and be thankful for His work in my life.

4. I will have a diminished sense of dependence upon Him as I share truth with others. This could result either in carelessness in my sharing with others, or accepting responsibility for another person's response, a weight that God never intended us to carry.

For Further Study

1. Scripture

Several passages in the Bible help us understand the Holy Spirit's role in salvation. They include:

- Psalm 32:3–5
- John 3:3–7
- John 14:16–17
- John 16:8–11
- Romans 6:1–10
- 1 Corinthians 1:13
- 1 Corinthians 6:19
- 2 Corinthians 1:22
- 2 Corinthians 5:17
- Ephesians 4:30
- Titus 3:5

2. Books

Several other books are very helpful in studying this subject. They are listed below in general order of difficulty. If I could read only one of them, I would read the first one.

Know What You Believe, Paul Little
The Mystery of the Holy Spirit, R. C. Sproul
Keep in Step with the Spirit, James I. Packer
Spirit-Filled: The Overflowing Power of the Holy Spirit, Jack Hayford (expresses the Pentecostal/charismatic view)

A humble, ignorant man or woman
depending on the mind of God has an
explanation for things that the rational man
without the Spirit of God never has.
■ Oswald Chambers (1874–1917)

4

How Does the Holy Spirit Help Me?

Helen Keller was born in the sleepy little town of Tuscumbia, Alabama, in 1880, to well-to-do, blue-blooded parents, Arthur Keller, a former Confederate officer, and Kate Adams, related to Robert E. Lee. A merciless illness ravaged Helen's body when she was only eighteen months old and left her sightless, deaf, and mute, trapping a brilliant mind inside a body that refused to exchange information with the outside world. It was like living in solitary confinement. The toll it took on her, mentally and emotionally, left her volatile and nearly uncontrollable as a young child. She grunted and gestured to try to communicate, but flew into a screaming rage when she was not understood.

Her brokenhearted parents grasped at every reasonable way to bring meaningful information into this starved little mind and unlock the little girl who lived inside. On the advice of Alexander Graham Bell, inventor of the telephone, her parents sent for a teacher from Boston who would change Helen's life and write a remarkable chapter of history. Her name was Anne Sullivan, who had herself been blind for a time. Her daunting task was to somehow penetrate the barrier of darkness and silence and "teach" Helen about a world she could neither see nor hear.

The early going was not encouraging. To Miss Sullivan's attempts to reach out to her, Helen responded with mean and spiteful behavior. Yet Anne kept pressing the one avenue she felt held hope: to teach Helen the "deaf" alphabet signs by "spelling" them into her hand. For example, she would give Helen a cup, and then put her hand in Helen's palm and spell the signing word "c-u-p," so that Helen could feel the shape of the letters she signed in her hand. At first this confused and frustrated Helen, because she perceived no relationship between the objects and the movement of Miss Sullivan's hands. The breakthrough came one day when Anne pumped water on Helen's hand while spelling w-a-t-e-r into her hand at the same time. The light began to dawn as Helen finally grasped that everything had its own name. No longer did she confuse the water with the cup or the pump. Like parched land starving for rain, Helen's mind soaked up the alphabet and vocabulary words until two years later she was reading and writing Braille fluently, as well as "signing" words with her hands.

Constant attention from Anne Sullivan helped Helen Keller's impressive mind expand to take in all Miss Sullivan could teach her. Then, in 1900, Miss Keller did the impossible. She went to Radcliffe, College, where Miss Sullivan "spelled" the lectures into her hand. Four years later, Helen graduated cum laude to worldwide acclaim. In the years that followed, Helen Keller became a member of an international community. She was personal friends with millionaire philanthropist Andrew Carnegie, authors Mark Twain and Robert Louis Stevenson, nearly every president who held office during her lifetime, and many famous people in the United States and around the globe.

In this chapter we learn that . . .

1. The Holy Spirit gives a Christian inner assurance of salvation.
2. The Holy Spirit divinely enables a Christian to understand Scripture in a way that he could not before becoming a Christian.
3. The Holy Spirit leads and guides Christians by putting it in our hearts and minds to do His will and by providentially governing our circumstances.
4. The Holy Spirit encourages and enables us to pray, and even prays to God the Father for us when we don't know what to pray.

She spent her life lecturing, raising money for the handicapped, writing, and traveling. She was truly a remarkable intellect. Yet none of this would have been possible without the nearly invisible Anne Sullivan. For fifty years, Miss Sullivan was at Helen's side teaching her, introducing her to all these people, translating and interpreting back and forth. It was Anne who spoke the actual words when Helen lectured. She made all their travel arrangements, making sure Helen arrived at appointments on time. Anne kept Helen's writing supplies handy, acting as personal secretary, valet, steward, and intimate friend. Helen Keller received all the public attention, but if it were not for the self-sacrificing ministry of Anne Sullivan, Helen might have grown up an "idiot," as such children were classified in those days, deprived and maladjusted, with no meaningful intercourse with society.

The ancient Greeks had a word that described Anne Sullivan. She was a *parakletos*, which meant someone who came alongside to help. She was a companion, helper, comforter. She was at Helen Keller's side at all times to make up for Helen's inherent deficiencies. She was more than a friend, because a friend might want to help but not be able to. She was more than an expert. One expert might be able to help but not want to. Anne wanted to help and she was able. Her entire goal in life was to make Helen Keller as successful as she could possibly be.

The writers of the New Testament used that same word to describe the Holy Spirit. He is our *parakletos*—our helper, our comforter, our companion. In John 14:16, we read, "And I will pray the Father, and He will give you another Helper [*parakletos*], that He may abide with you forever." It means, literally, called to one's side, to one's aid, and suggests the adaptability for giving aid. The word also was used in a court of justice to denote a legal assistant, an advocate, an intercessor, one who pleads another's cause. In the widest sense, it signifies a helper and comforter.

Why I need to know this:

1. To have a biblical view of the ministry of the Holy Spirit.
2. To benefit from His ministry to me and not miss out on anything due to my ignorance.
3. To be able correctly to represent the ministry of the Holy Spirit to others.

What Anne Sullivan was to Helen Keller, the Holy Spirit is to us, and more. After reviewing the ways Miss Sullivan helped Miss Keller, now we want to look at the ways the Holy Spirit helps us. The Holy Spirit helps us by giving us assurance of our salvation, by teaching us the things of God, by leading and guiding us in life, and by praying for us.

How Does the Holy Spirit Make the Christian Feel Secure?

The Holy Spirit gives a Christian inner assurance of salvation.

Central Passage: Romans 8:16, THE SPIRIT HIMSELF BEARS WITNESS WITH OUR SPIRIT THAT WE ARE CHILDREN OF GOD.

There are few things more plaguing than *wanting* to be a

Christian and not being sure you *are* one. I have already told you of the night I became a Christian. I was told that the Holy Spirit would indwell me, and I had a mental picture of a Max-shaped spirit who would merge with my physical outline, like two camera images coming into focus as one. When it didn't "feel" as though that happened, I went away unsure I was really a Christian. That was complicated by the fact that, by faith, I told a Christian friend of mine that I had become a Christian. My friend asked me a couple of questions, and then said, "I don't think you are a Christian." This friend had some pretty stringent requirements for what it took to be a Christian—more than the Bible had, I later learned—and I didn't measure up. That shook me.

My already fragile confidence was shattered. The final blow came one night when I shouted myself awake. As a new Christian, I had begun attending a Christian college that taught the doctrine that Jesus would come back within sight of earth, there would be a loud shout and the sound of a trumpet, and all Christians would immediately be taken to heaven (1 Thessalonians 4:16–17). It would be the beginning of the end of history on earth. With this remarkable newly acquired knowledge, I went to sleep in my dormitory room one Friday night, and I did something I had never done before and have never done since. For no reason whatever, I shouted very loud right in the middle of my sleep. I was not dreaming. And it was not one of those long, low moaning sounds you make when you are dreaming and think you are shouting. I shouted! I sat bolt upright in bed, as though I had been pulled erect by some invisible hand. It was the dead of night. Not a sound came from the normally noisy hall. When I got up and looked out the window, I could see no sign of life. For some strange reason I talked myself into connecting my shout with the shout in 1 Thessalonians 4:16–17 and convinced myself that the Lord had come for the Christians and I had missed it. My roommate was still asleep, but that was no comfort. I didn't know him very well. Maybe he was not a Christian!

Uncertainty about your salvation can be agonizing.

I spent several agonizing hours reading my Bible and praying, asking God to come and get me if He had missed me the first time. I believed in Him and wanted to go to heaven. After finally drifting off into some fitful sleep, the sun came up, the campus came alive with students, and I concluded that that many people on a Christian campus couldn't have missed it too, and my Great

Shout must have had no connection with the prophecy in 1 Thessalonians.

As a result of this rather shaky start, for a number of years I was a little weak on assurance of salvation. This was particularly acute whenever I had to fly. It was white-knuckle time from take-off to landing. Turbulence had a dramatic effect on me. The slightest bump caused my heart to race, my breath to become short. On the outside, I looked calm and unflappable. On the inside, I was shouting, "Oh, God, if you get me off this plane, I'll never get on a plane again as long as I live." But then, the plane would land, everything I had felt and said seemed pretty silly, and eventually I'd get on a plane again, to a repeat performance.

The Holy Spirit definitely had an uphill battle with me. But, true to His word, He won. He assured me that I was a Christian. First, I read 2 Corinthians 5:17, "If anyone is in Christ, he is a new creation; old things have passed away; behold, all things have become new." I had noticed a number of my more flagrant sins had, without conscious effort on my part, disappeared. I thought that was significant. Then, when I read the Corinthians passage, something deep down inside me shouted, "That's why. I've become a new creation. Old things have passed away, and all things have become new." I'm not sure I had an accurate understanding of the passage, but I began to gain assurance anyway.

A new creation does things differently.

Then, I put several passages together that convinced me even more:

1. "There is forgiveness with You" (Psalm 130:4). This gave me hope. It meant forgiveness could be obtained from God.
2. "The one who comes to Me I will by no means cast out" (John 6:37). I had come to Him; there was no doubt about that. I had repented of my sin and asked Jesus to forgive my sin, to come into my life and make me the kind of person He wanted me to be and give me eternal life so I could live with Him in heaven. Since I had come to Him, and He had promised He would not cast me out, clearly I had Jesus.
3. "He who has the Son has life" (1 John 5:12). Because I had the Son, I had eternal life.

The Holy Spirit used these passages to convince me that I was, indeed, a Christian. I finally gained assurance of my salvation through the ministry of the Holy Spirit.

Giving us assurance of our salvation is one of the ministries the Holy Spirit has to us. In Romans 8:15–17, we read, "For you did not receive the spirit of bondage again to fear [when you became Christians], but you received the Spirit of adoption by whom we cry out 'Abba, Father,' The Spirit Himself bears witness with our spirit that we are children of God, and if children, then heirs—heirs of God and joint heirs with Christ, if indeed we suffer with Him, that we may also be glorified together." We gain an inner assurance that we are children of God, and that inner assurance comes from the Holy Spirit. Beyond that, I don't know that we can say *how* He does it, or if He does it in the same way with each person. In my case, He gave me a clearer understanding of some Scripture passages, which led me to assurance.

Assurance comes through the Holy Spirit.

How Does the Holy Spirit Teach the Christian?

The Holy Spirit divinely enables a Christian to understand Scripture in a way that he could not before becoming a Christian.

Central Passage: 1 Corinthians 2:13, *These things we also speak, not in words which man's wisdom teaches but which the Holy Spirit teaches.*

I struggled spiritually for many months before I became a Christian. I was frustrated with a lack of purpose and meaning in life, I was under terrible guilt for sins I was committing, and I was terribly fearful of dying, because I figured I would go to hell when I died. In my tormented condition, I picked up an old family Bible and tried to read it, but I couldn't make heads or tails of it. It was like trying to read a book on nonsense. I spoke English and the Bible I was reading was written in English, but I got absolutely nothing out of it.

Then, on September 1, 1966, I became a Christian; and the man who led me to the Lord gave me a paperback New Testament and encouraged me to read the Gospel of John several times. When I picked up the Bible this time, it came alive with meaning. I couldn't get enough of it. I read it over and over, every spare minute I had. I didn't understand everything I read, but I was ecstatic with what I did understand. So I read and read, not worrying about what I didn't understand, just trying to increase my knowledge of what I did.

I'm not suggesting everyone will experience this kind of difference upon conversion. But it is an example of the illumining ministry of the Holy Spirit. What was the difference between the first and second times I tried to read the Bible? The second time I had the Holy Spirit living inside me, teaching me, opening my mind to the truth of Scripture, helping me understand. In 1 Corinthians 2:9–10 we read:

> "Eye has not seen, nor ear heard,
> Nor have entered into the heart of man
> The things which God has prepared for those who love Him."
> But God has revealed them to us through His Spirit.

There we have it. God reveals things to us through His Spirit that we would not know otherwise. He enables us to understand and apply what He has already revealed in the Scriptures. The pull to sin that is within each of us clouds our minds and our wills so that we misunderstand, misinterpret, and resist the full truth of Scripture. We lack both the ability and the inclination to understand. The Holy Spirit, however, opens our minds and warms our hearts so that we have a growing understanding and a growing inclination to follow Scripture (Ephesians 1:17–18; 3:18–19; 2 Corinthians 3:14–16; 4:6). It may not be as sudden and clear-cut as my experience, but the Holy Spirit *will* open the mind of the Christian to the truth of Scripture. David prayed again and again, especially in Psalm 119, that the Lord would teach Him. "Deal bountifully with Your servant, that I may live and keep Your word. Open my eyes, that I may see wondrous things from Your law" (vv. 17–18). That is a prayer we all can pray. It is a prayer God delights in answering.

How Does the Holy Spirit Lead and Guide Us?

The Holy Spirit leads and guides Christians by putting it in our hearts and minds to do His will and by providentially governing our circumstances.

Central Passage: Philippians 2:12–13, *Work out your own salvation with fear and trembling; for it is God who works in you both to will and to do for His good pleasure.*

How to know the will of God can be one of the great challenges of the Christian life, and often one of the great frustrations of the young Christian life. The young Christian, in his zeal, wants God to let him know everything that He should do, and God doesn't do that. God's will in the New Testament is primarily moral. He wants us to "be" the right kind of people. If we are the right kind of people, God will find it easy to lead us to do whatever He wants us to do. Typically, however, we are preoccupied with what God wants us to *do*, comfortable just *being* the kind of person God wants us to be, and resting in His sovereignty to determine what we should do.

Nevertheless, the Bible does indicate that God will lead us and guide us, even though we may not feel led or guided. Romans 8:14 says, "For as many as are led by the Spirit of God, these are the sons of God." Galatians 5:16, 18 reads, "Walk in the Spirit, and you shall not fulfill the lust of the flesh. But if you are led by the Spirit, you are not under the law." So we see that we are led by the Spirit, or can be, but how? What does that mean?

While we want to *do*, God wants us to *be*.

Of course, the easiest way to be led is by providentially governed circumstances. If circumstances prohibit you from doing something, you know it is not the will of God. He is not leading you into someplace where He makes it impossible to go.

The next easiest way He leads is through Scripture. The Holy Spirit may make a passage of the Bible known to us, and that may lead us or guide us.

A further way is through the counsel of others. Proverbs teaches that there is safety in the multitude of counselors. It takes a brave or foolish person to go counter to an abundance of solid, wise counsel.

Finally, apparently God plants inclinations, thoughts, or desires in our mind to lead and guide us. This is the most subjective and the most dangerous, because it is often difficult to know whether something in our head is our own personal desire, or perhaps even a deception by the evil one. In such a case, it is helpful simply to retrace the above principles. First, do circumstances tell us anything? If you try to go through a door that has been closed by God, you often end up with a sore head. An apparently closed door is not always an indication of the Lord's

will, however. It may be for faith-building, or to make sure the
timing is right. Second, does the Scripture tell us anything? Third,
is there agreement on an abundance of godly wisdom and counsel?

Finally, if you have followed these steps and you still don't
sense any direct leading or guiding from the Lord, you are free to
do as you please. The great reformer Martin Luther said, "Love
God and do as you please." Of course, this
could easily be misunderstood or abused. But
what he meant was, if you love God, you
will obey His commandments. The apostle
John wrote, "If you love Me, you will keep My commandments"
(John 14:15, NASB). If you disobey His commandments, at
least for that moment, you have stopped loving God. If you love
God, you will not do anything that you understand to be
wrong.

If you love God, you want to please Him.

Philip Yancey wrote, in a little booklet entitled *Guidance:*

I have a confession to make. For me, at least, guidance only
becomes evident when I look backward, months and years later.
Then the circuitous process falls into place and the hand of God
seems clear. But at that moment of decision, I feel mainly confu-
sion and uncertainty. Indeed, almost all the guidance in my life
has been subtle and indirect.

This pattern has recurred so often (and clear guidance for the
future has occurred so seldom) that I am about to conclude that
we have a basic direction wrong. I had always thought of guidance as forward-looking. We keep praying, hoping, counting on
God to reveal what we should do next. In my own experience, at
least, I have found the direction to be reversed. The focus must be
on the moment before me, the present. How is my relationship to
God? As circumstances change, for better or worse, will I respond
with obedience and trust?

God does guide—sometimes through an inner conviction,
sometimes through circumstances, sometimes through Scripture
or godly counsel. But sometimes we don't have any sense of being led or guided. That does not mean we aren't. It means we are
free to love God and do as we please, and wait to see, in retrospect, what the will of God was.

How Does the Holy Spirit Help Us Pray?

The Holy Spirit encourages and enables us to pray, and even prays to God the Father for us when we don't know what to pray.

Central Passage: Romans 8:26–27, *The Spirit also helps in our weaknesses. For we do not know what we should pray for as we ought, but the Spirit Himself makes intercession for us with groanings which cannot be uttered. Now* [God the Father] *who searches the hearts knows what the mind of the Spirit is, because* [the Spirit] *makes intercession for the saints according to the will of God.*

In a *Peanuts* cartoon many years ago, Linus told Lucy, "I've made an important theological discovery. If you hold your hands upside down when you pray, you get the opposite of what you prayed for."

Many of us read that and think, "So that's what's the matter with my prayers. I've been holding my hands upside down!" Certainly there are times when we get the opposite of what we prayed for. Prayer is one of the most difficult problems in the Christian life.

The Bible suggests that the Holy Spirit encourages us and guides us in our prayer (Ephesians 6:18; Jude 20). Yet there are times, the Bible says, when we do not know how to pray as we should (Romans 8:26, NASB), but we already knew that from experience. First, the Bible says whatever we ask in Jesus' name, it will be given to us (John 14:13). But then, it says we must ask in faith without doubting (James 1:6), without unconfessed sin (John 9:31), and in God's will (1 John 5:14). Well, what if we don't know what God's will is? What do we do then?

Our purpose in this chapter is not to answer all the questions we might have about prayer. Rather, our purpose is to make this point: The Holy Spirit wants us to pray, encourages us to pray, guides us in prayer, and when we do not know what to pray for, the Holy Spirit takes up our cause and prays to the Father for us. Therefore, we should never fear praying to God or be discouraged about our prayer. Rather, we can go to God and admit that we don't know how to pray for something as we ought, and rest in the confidence that the Holy Spirit will make the proper prayer on our behalf. What freedom that gives us! We can just pray, with a free heart, knowing that the Holy

We can pray freely, knowing the Holy Spirit is praying for us.

Spirit is praying for us at the same time, translating our mixed-up thoughts, our uncertainty and ignorance, into valid, meaningful prayers.

The Scripture makes it clear that we are not to pray with selfish motives (James 4:3), or with sin in our heart (Psalm 66:18), or without faith (James 1:6). At the same time, God readily hears the prayer, "Lord, I have sinned. Forgive my sin, and restore me to fellowship with you." If we have taken care of those matters, we can pray. So pray. Risk praying poorly. Pray the best you know how. The Holy Spirit is there, translating, interpreting, praying to the Father for you.

Speed Bump!

Slow down to be sure you've gotten the main points of this chapter.

*Q*uestion
*A*nswer

Q1. How does the Holy Spirit make the Christian feel secure?

A1. The Holy Spirit gives a Christian inner *assurance* of salvation.

Q2. How does the Holy Spirit teach the Christian?

A2. The Holy Spirit divinely enables a Christian to *understand* Scripture in a way that he could not before becoming a Christian.

Q3. How does the Holy Spirit lead and guide us?

A3. The Holy Spirit leads and guides Christians by putting it in our hearts and minds to do His *will* and by providentially governing our circumstances.

Q4. How does the Holy Spirit help us pray?

A4. The Holy Spirit encourages and enables us to pray, and even prays to God the Father *for* us when we don't know what to pray.

Fill in the Blank

*Q*uestion
*A*nswer

Q1. How does the Holy Spirit make the Christian feel secure?

A1. The Holy Spirit gives a Christian inner _____ of salvation.

Q2. How does the Holy Spirit teach the Christian?

A2. The Holy Spirit divinely enables a Christian to _____ Scripture in a way that he could not before becoming a Christian.

Q3. How does the Holy Spirit lead and guide us?

A3. The Holy Spirit leads and guides Christians by putting it in our hearts and minds to do His _____ and by providentially governing our circumstances.

Q4. How does the Holy Spirit help us pray?

A4. The Holy Spirit encourages and enables us to pray, and even prays to God the Father _____ us when we don't know what to pray.

For Further Thought and Discussion

1. Have you ever had anyone come alongside you in your life and help you when you really needed it? How did it make you feel? How does it affect your mental image of the Holy Spirit to know that He does that continuously for you, even though you are usually not aware of it?

2. Do you have an inner assurance that you are a Christian based on Scripture? What Scripture would you use to support that conviction if you have it? If you do not have such a conviction, do you think it is because you are not a Christian, or is there some other reason?

3. We all have trouble understanding parts of Scripture, and there are parts that we will not understand this side of heaven. But do you receive enough insight, comfort, guidance, and motivation from Scripture to convince you that the Holy Spirit is teaching you? If you do, could you give an example? If not, what do you think is the most likely reason?

4. What is an example of a time God led you through inner prompting that proved (in retrospect, as Yancey described) to be the will of God? Give an additional example of God's leading you through external circumstances.

What If I Don't Believe?

1. I may miss out on some of the ministry the Holy Spirit would like to have in my life.

2. I have a sub-biblical understanding and view of the Holy Spirit.

3. I miss out on the peace and joy of knowing that the third person of the Trinity is on a constant watch for my welfare.

4. I have little to share with others regarding this subject.

For Further Study

1. Scripture
Several passages in the Bible are central to understanding how the Holy Spirit helps us. They include:

- Psalm 119:17–18
- Romans 8:14–16
- Romans 8:26–27
- 1 Corinthians 2:6–10
- 2 Corinthians 3:14–16
- 2 Corinthians 4:6
- Galatians 5:16–18
- Ephesians 1:17–18
- Ephesians 3:18–19
- Philippians 2:12–13
- 1 John 2:27

2. Books
Several other books are very helpful in studying this subject. They are listed below in general order of difficulty. If I could read only one of them, I would read the first one:

A Survey of Bible Doctrine, Charles Ryrie
Essential Truths of the Christian Faith, R. C. Sproul
The Holy Spirit, Billy Graham

*Without the present illumination of the Holy
Spirit, the Word of God must remain a dead
letter to every man, no matter how intelligent
or well-educated he may be. . . . It is just as
essential for the Holy Spirit to reveal the
truth of Scripture to the reader today as it
was necessary for him to inspire the writers
in their day.*
■ William Law (1686–1761)

5

How Does the Holy Spirit Change Me?

The frog was lucky. When the princess kissed him, there was a loud "FFffooooff!" A cloud of smoke rose toward the heavens, and the frog was gone. In his place stood a handsome young prince with golden, wavy hair, a Grecian profile, straight white teeth, and square jaw. He was the picture of perfection. The princess swooned. He picked her up in his powerful arms and carried her effortlessly to his white charger, mounted swiftly, and raced off toward the castle on the horizon.

His change was instantaneous, complete, and permanent. He didn't have to struggle to change the way we do. If frogs were changed into princes the way Christians are changed into the spiritual image of Christ, we would see quite a different story. The non-Christian frog would be "kissed," as it were, by Jesus. There would a slight *pfzzt*, a little wisp of smoke would curl upward, and where the frog once stood would now stand a curious mixture of frog and prince. We'd have to call him a *frince*. He has a handsome head with a golden crown, gleaming white teeth, a winsome smile, strong broad shoulders, with well-muscled arms, and a torso squatting on two green, mottled, warted legs tucked awkwardly under him. He might say something like, "It behooves me on this auspicious occasion to *rribit, rribit*."

The transformation was permanent but not instantaneous or complete. And that's not all. Two months later, we see a frog with a green, mottled, warted human face with a cocked crown on its head. The frince has lost ground. He is not even as far along now as he was when he first became a Christian. However, over the next year, he gradually gains ground. He gets his human head, shoulders, and arms back, and even has human legs; but he is still pretty green, says "*rribit*" more than he ought to, and just when you think he should be past it, he goes out and eats a huge, disgusting, green and purple fly.

Five years later, he seems pretty much the same, only not quite as green, nor quite as many warts. However, his pace of change has slowed. He has not changed as much, per year, in the last four years as he did the first. In fact, when his work is frustrating, when he has a fight with his wife, when the kids drive him nuts, or his boss humiliates him, he might be found back on a lily pad looking almost totally like a frog again, eating flies and bugs, drinking murky water, croaking flatly, and staring sightlessly into the night. This is not the experience with all frinces. Some make better progress than others.

No, the fairy tale frog was lucky. Real life for the Christian is not so easy. Our change from a frog to a prince is a gradual transformation, and not an unbroken, uphill progression. Rather, it is like a stock-market chart. Some days up, some days down, but overall, we hope, an upward movement.

In this chapter we learn that . . .

1. The goal of spiritual change is transformation into the spiritual likeness of Jesus.
2. At the heart of spiritual change is an interaction in which the Holy Spirit prompts and the individual responds.
3. To become like Christ requires the combination of the work of God, the word of God, personal commitment, other believers, and time and trials.
4. We don't change more quickly and more completely because God has decreed that we be transformed over time and because of the complications of sin.

This can be pretty unnerving for us. We all want to be more than we are, but we aren't sure how. Remember that, spiritually, one's reach always exceeds his grasp. When traveling one can always see farther down the road than where he is at any moment. You see mountains off in the distance, but you are not there yet. After many minutes of driving, you get to those mountains, but now there are other mountains off in the distance.

The same thing is true spiritually. The spiritual life is a journey, and you can always see farther down the road spiritually than you currently are. For that reason, the Christian life is often haunted by dissatisfaction at best, and deep travail at worst. In the better moments of one's spiritual pilgrimage, the Christian is gratified with the spiritual growth God has granted, enriched by the communion of the Lord and the fellowship of other saints. Yet even in these good moments, the believer knows that there is more. The character gulf between him and Jesus is still there. Like geese in November that are unsettled until they finally head south for the winter, so the Christian is unsettled and drawn inexorably beyond the ground on which he stands, toward the warmer climate of fuller fellowship with Christ.

Then there are other moments in the Christian experience when, like Peter after he denied Jesus, we rush out into the darkness and weep bitterly. We wonder how Jesus can forgive us so great a sin, or a sin committed so often. We wonder when we will finally be rid of that weakness, that propensity that mars the image of Christ stamped on our lives. "Why, by now, have I not left that sin behind me?" we wonder. "Why, when I thought I had victory over that sin, has it reared again its monstrous head to mock and torment me? How long, O Lord, will your servant be plagued by the hounds of hell biting at my heels when I should have far outrun them by now?"

If there were a button we could push, and by doing so never sin again, would we not rush for the button to push it? On the surface, we all sin because we choose to, and in that sense, because we want to. But below the surface, we don't want to sin. Part of the new birth is a longing to be unblemished in our motives, attitudes, behavior, and words. The new man within cries out to be holy in all his behavior, because the God we serve is holy (1 Peter 1:15).

It is not that we see no progress. In fact, in some areas of our lives we may see more progress than we expected. But other areas seem impossible to stamp out. Like the great mythical phoenix, every time we think our sins have crashed and burned, a new bird rises from the ashes to plague us again.

How do we leave deeply rooted sin behind? How do we escape the attitudes, values, and behavior of the past? How does the Holy Spirit change us? What is the process? Why does it take so long to be holy? How will the longing in our hearts to be "at one" with Jesus be fulfilled? These are deep questions that have even deeper answers that we can only touch upon.

What Is the Goal of Spiritual Change?

The goal of spiritual change is transformation into the spiritual likeness of Jesus.

Central Passage: 2 Corinthians 3:18, *But we all, with unveiled face, beholding as in a mirror the glory of the Lord, are being transformed into the same image from glory to glory, just as by the Spirit of the Lord.*

An old proverb says, "The apple never falls far from the tree." It means that children are often like their parents, both physically and in some nonphysical characteristics. God also wants us to not fall far from His tree. His goal for us as Christians is that we be changed from our pre-Christian nature into the likeness of Jesus. In our central passage, we see that we are being transformed by the Spirit of the Lord into the image of Jesus. Romans 12:1–2 says essentially the same thing: "I beseech you therefore, brethren, by the mercies of God, that you present your bodies a living sacrifice, holy, acceptable to God, which is your reasonable service. And do not be conformed to this world, but be transformed by the renewing of your mind, that you may prove what is that good and acceptable and perfect will of God."

To understand this passage better, try working it backwards. If we want to be a living demonstration (proof) of the fact that God's will is good and acceptable and perfect, we must be transformed. To be transformed, we must have our mind renewed. To have our mind renewed, we must present ourselves to God as a living sacrifice.

This, then, is our goal—the spiritual likeness of Jesus. What is the spiritual likeness of Jesus? You are to love God with "all your heart, with all your soul, and with all your mind. This is the first and great commandment. And the second is like it: You shall love your neighbor as yourself." That is the opening picture of what it means to be like Jesus. It means you love God and your fellowman.

You might ask, however, how you love God. The Gospel of John answers that clearly: "If you love me, keep My commandments" (John 14:15). The essence of loving God is not sweeping emotions or lofty intentions; it is obedience. Regardless of our emotions or our good intentions, if we do not keep God's commandments, we cannot say we love Him. By this I do not mean a casual type of obedience, but. obedience from the heart because we believe God always has our best in mind.

Two other passages help give us a picture of the image of Jesus and a glimpse of what it means to love our neighbor. One is 1 Corinthians 13:4–7: "Love suffers long and is kind; love does not envy; love does not parade itself, is not puffed up; does not behave rudely, does not seek its own, is not provoked, thinks no evil; does not rejoice in iniquity, but rejoices in the truth." That is what it means to love others.

To let this passage have its full impact, put your own name in the blank, in place of the word "love." (*Your name*) suffers long and is kind; _____ does not envy; _____ does not parade [himself], is not puffed up; _____ does not behave rudely, does not seek his own, is not provoked, thinks no evil; _____ does not rejoice in iniquity, but rejoices in the truth. How did you do? How close are you to the image of Christ using *this* passage as a yardstick?

We also need to look at Galatians 5:22–23: "The fruit of the Spirit is love, joy, peace, longsuffering, kindness, goodness, faithfulness, gentleness, self-control."

These passages together do not give us the total picture, but they put us well on our way to understanding what it means to be like Jesus. We love God and we love others. It's a big task.

What Is at the Heart of Spiritual Change?

At the heart of spiritual change is an interaction in which the Holy Spirit prompts and the individual responds.

Central Passage: Philippians 2:12–13, *Work out your own salvation with fear and trembling; for it is God who works in you both to will and to do for His good pleasure.*

Like many things in the Bible, spiritual growth can seem fairly simple on the surface, but when you plumb the depths, it becomes extremely complex. While we may never understand everything about spiritual change in the Christian, our central passage in Philippians suggests that God places a thought or desire in our mind—it may be a conviction that something we have done is wrong, or that we ought to do something positive—and we either respond or reject that thought or desire. If we nourish

His divine "seed," that encourages more, and if we extinguish it, that encourages less.

The Holy Spirit may put into our mind a command from Scripture as we are tempted to sin. He may give us an impulse to do something kind for someone in need. It might be a feeling of remorse over something we said, and a conviction that we ought to ask for forgiveness. If we respond positively to that inner prompting, we are strengthened by the Spirit for the next test. If we respond negatively, we are weakened by our flesh (Romans 7:18–25) for the next test. If we develop a habit of responding positively, we develop a strong Christian character. Negative responses lead to a weak Christian character. On the surface, it seems as simple as that.

Below the surface, it is much more complicated, however, because our ability to understand Scripture is a result of the work of the Holy Spirit in our lives (1 Corinthians 2:9–15). Furthermore, our ability to bear any fruit in the Christian life is dependent on Jesus ("for without Me you can do nothing"—John 15:5).

Ephesians 2:8–9 says, "For by grace you have been saved through faith, and that not of yourselves; it is the gift of God, not of works, lest anyone should boast." The question we must ask about this passage is, "To what does the 'that' refer?" Does it mean the grace to be saved is not of ourselves? Or does it mean the faith to be saved is not of ourselves? The word nearest to "that" is "faith." Normally, the word "that" refers to the thing closest to it. So, if the passage teaches that even the faith to be saved is not of ourselves, but is a gift of God, it only adds to the mystery of spiritual growth. If that which we need to be saved and grow spiritually is given us by God, how, then, can be we held accountable to be more than we are, spiritually? And yet, the Bible holds us accountable for our spiritual growth (Romans 6:1–14).

We cannot solve the mystery. All we can do is live in the light of what we understand. We understand this much: God somehow puts thoughts, desires, Scriptures, convictions, or impulses into our minds ("it is God who works in you both to will and to do for His good pleasure"). We are responsible to act properly on them ("work out your own salvation with fear and trembling"). When we do, God increases our capacity to respond positively the next time. When we don't, our capacity to respond positively the next time is diminished. As we say "yes" to God, He makes us stronger spiritually. As we say "no" to Him, we make selves weaker.

The principle of Matthew 25:15–29 makes it clear that light received brings more light, and light rejected brings greater darkness; obedience now makes greater obedience possible in the future.

How do we grow, spiritually? The grace of God is the basis of all spiritual growth. But, because we do not have the luxury of being totally passive in this process, it is helpful to observe how God sometimes works in our lives. The Holy Spirit puts something in our mind. We respond positively, as best we know how, as fully as we are able. The Lord accepts our positive heart response as a proper act of faith and enables us to respond on a level that He determines. This strengthens us for greater response next time. His grace makes possible our obedience and our growth.

The fruit of the Spirit, we learn in Galatians 5:22–23, is love, joy, peace, longsuffering, kindness, goodness, faithfulness, gentleness, and self-control. If these are the fruits of the Spirit, they are not the fruit of self-effort. That means that we cannot create them in our own lives. The Holy Spirit must create them. Yet, the Holy Spirit will not create this fruit in our lives unless we are pursuing the things that encourage this fruit.

In his book, *True Spirituality*, Francis Schaeffer coined the phrase "active passivity" to describe this spiritual interaction between the Holy Spirit who prompts and the individual who responds. We are active and passive at the same time. We are active in response to the things God asks of us. We are passive in that all the results are His.

Having said all that, we should be aware of the danger inherent in following inner impulses, namely that you might get an inner impulse that is not from God. Where would the impulse come from? Two sources are possible: the human mind or demonic forces. The human mind, unaided by the Holy Spirit, can create inner impulses. Non-Christians have "hunches" all the time. Also, it is clear that the devil is capable of moving us to do things (1 Chronicles 21:1). So we must not blindly follow our inner impulses.

Early in my ministry I knew of a lady with a painful and chronic condition who became a Christian. She prayed to God continuously to take the pain away. One day, it came into her mind that she should go to a certain drugstore in the city that was unknown to her. She was to ask the druggist for a certain kind of medication that, again, was unknown to her. She did these things. But the druggist told her that medicine was not even manufactured anymore. The woman was crushed. She felt God had lied to her. She turned from God, and though this was many years ago, the last I knew, she was still rejecting the Lord.

Why I need to know this

1. If I don't know that transformation into the spiritual image of Jesus is God's primary goal for me, I may misunderstand His work in my life, especially wondering why He does not make life easier for His follower.

2. If I don't understand that spiritual growth is an interaction between me and the Holy Spirit, I may fall into one of two errors. I may put too much emphasis on my own responsibility, or, I may put too much responsibility on God's sovereignty.

3. If I don't understand all the elements of God's spiritual transformation process, I may leave out one or more in my mind, and either stunt my spiritual growth or get frustrated because I don't understand why my growth isn't progressing more quickly.

What went wrong with that experience? How is someone to know if an inner impulse is from God or not? Well, frankly, it is like much of life. The will of God becomes clear after the fact, not before. There are many times when we do not know what the will of God is. We make the best decision we know how at the time, and later we gain perspective. Someone once observed, "Life is lived forward, but understood backward."

Several principles can help us evaluate our inner impulses.

1. One of my pastors early in my Christian experience often said, "Follow your *good* impulses. It is probably the Holy Spirit." If the impulse is to do something good, there is little danger in doing it. In fact, it really doesn't matter if the impulse is directly from the Holy Spirit or indirectly from God through your spiritually influenced mind, if good is the result. We are to do good to others anyway (Galatians 6:10).

2. Sometimes the impulse is to do something that seems neither good nor bad. If it is a small thing, it is not necessary to agonize over it. Do it if you want to. In 1 Corinthians 10:27, Paul wrote, "If any of those who do not believe invites you to dinner, and you desire to go, eat whatever is set before you, asking no

question for conscience' sake." It does not say "Pray about it, get counsel from ten people, and then wait twenty-four hours before making your final decision." It simply says, "If you want to go, go."

If it is a big thing, then you will want to pray about it, seek counsel, search the Scriptures, and make a pro and con list. Don't do any big thing hastily.

3. Trust in the character of God. The woman who turned her back on God over the drugstore incident, revealed a deep flaw in her understanding of God. If you believe that God is all-good, all-powerful, and all-knowing, then you can trust Him. The proper response to that lady's inner impulse might have been to go to the drugstore and ask for the medicine, but when she learned that the medicine was no longer manufactured, to cast herself on God's character and admit that the process of inner impulses is an imperfect one, or to admit that the inner impulse might have just come from her subconscious mind. The impulse might also have come as a test from Satan, in which case prayer to the Lord for protection from his deception would be in order.

I think that the more spiritually mature a person is, the more he can trust such impulses. The less mature he is, the more caution should be exercised. In all cases, caution is the watchword.

What Process Must We Go Through to Become Like Christ?

To become like Christ requires the combination of the work of God, the word of God, personal commitment, other believers, and time and trials.

Central Passage: Romans 12:1–2. *I beseech you therefore, brethren, by the mercies of God, that you present your bodies a living sacrifice, holy, acceptable to God, which is your reasonable service. And do not be conformed to this world, but be transformed by the renewing of your mind, that you may prove what is that good and acceptable and perfect will of God.*

Five key ingredients are required for someone to develop a mature Christian character. I deal with these more fully in my book, *30 Days to Understanding How To Live as a Christian,* so I will summarize them here. They are the work of God, the word of God, other believers, and time and trials.

The Work of God

As we saw earlier, it is God who works in us "both to will and to do for His good pleasure." Someone has said, "God does the work of God, and man does the work of man. Man cannot do the work of God, and God will not do the work of man." If that is the case, we must be clear about what is the work of God and what is our responsibility. We have a great genius for turning the two around. We prefer to try to do the work of God and neglect the work of man. It doesn't work. We must look to God to initiate the work in our hearts, and we must respond with faithful obedience.

The Word of God

Transformation cannot be complete without the word of God. Without the Bible, we don't know what we should do, and the Holy Spirit does not have His key tool in our lives. The writer of the book of Hebrews wrote: "[God's word] is full of living power: it is sharper than the sharpest dagger, cutting swift and deep into our innermost thoughts and desires . . . exposing us for what we really are" (4:12, LB).

The Scripture has inherent power as it is used by the Holy Spirit in our lives. The apostle Paul wrote: "All Scripture is given by inspiration of God, and is profitable for doctrine, for reproof, for correction, for instruction in righteousness, that the man of God may be complete, thoroughly equipped for every good work" (2 Timothy 3:16–17).

David wrote in the Psalms, "How can a young man cleanse his way? By taking heed according to Your word. . . . Your word I have hidden in my heart, that I might not sin against You. . . . Your word is a lamp to my feet and a light to my path" (Psalm 119:9, 11, 105). He also wrote, in Psalm 19, that the word of God was more valuable than gold, sweeter than honey, and by it "Your servant is warned, and in keeping them there is great reward."

Without the Scriptures, no one has a hope of always making wise decisions, of consistently discerning the will of God, of knowing how to sustain relationships, of having a morally tuned conscience, of knowing right from wrong in the small as well as great areas of life, of knowing God well and worshiping Him in spirit and in truth, or of being equipped to live and minister in this world. In addition to the work of God, it takes the word of God to become spiritually mature.

Personal Commitment

Spiritual growth requires personal commitment. As we have already seen, spiritual growth is an interaction between the Christian and the Holy Spirit. The Christian cannot be totally passive in the process. God will not pull a Christian out of bed in the morning, splash cold water in his face, brew him a cup of coffee, and sit him down in front of his Bible. The Christian must do that himself. We must be personally involved in the pursuit of righteousness. Paul wrote in 1 Corinthians 9:24–27, "Do you not know that those who run in a race all run, but one receives the prize? Run in such a way that you may obtain it. And everyone who competes for the prize is temperate in all things. Now they do it to obtain a perishable crown, but we for an imperishable crown. Therefore I run thus: not with uncertainty. Thus I fight: not as one who beats the air. But I discipline my body and bring it into subjection, lest, when I have preached to others, I myself should become disqualified." Yes, personal commitment is one key to spiritual transformation.

Other Believers

Spiritual transformation does not happen in isolation. We need the ministry of other believers in our lives. The Christian life was never designed to be lived in isolation. The Lone Ranger is not a role model for Christians. The Three Musketeers would be more like it—all for one and one for all. The apostle Paul wrote in Ephesians 4:11–13, 15–16,

> And He Himself gave some to be apostles, some prophets, some evangelists, and some pastors and teachers, for the equipping of the saints for the work of ministry, for the edifying of the body of Christ, till we all come to the unity of the faith and of the knowledge of the Son of God, to a perfect man, to the measure of the stature of the fullness of Christ . . . but, speaking the truth in love, [we] may grow up in all things into Him who is the head—Christ—from whom the whole body, joined and knit together by what every joint supplies, according to the effective working by which every part does its share, causes growth of the body for the edifying of itself in love.

We are gifted and called by God to live a life intertwined with other Christians, so that we can all help one another grow to spiritual maturity. We cannot do it alone. God has seen to that.

Time and Trials

Finally, time and trials are necessary for spiritual transformation. No one was ever holy in a hurry. Paul writes in 1 Timothy that an elder must not be a new convert, lest he become conceited and fall into the snare of the devil (3:6, NASB). Peter calls new Christians "babes" and declares that they must drink milk in order to grow spiritually, to the point at which they can begin to eat solid food (Hebrews 5:12–14). All this implies that, when compared with physical growth, spiritual transformation takes time.

It also takes trials. No one ever grew to maturity on a cloud of ease. In fact, the writer of the book of Hebrews speaks of the need for God's children to be disciplined, just as earthly fathers discipline earthly children, and that if we do not receive discipline from God, it is a sign that we are not His children (Hebrews 12:8). He goes on to say that "no chastening seems to be joyful for the present, but painful; nevertheless afterward it yields the peaceable fruit of righteousness to those who have been trained by it" (12:11).

In a similar line of thought, the apostle James wrote, "My brethren, count it all joy when [*not if*] you fall into various trials, knowing that the testing of your faith produces patience. But let patience have its perfect work, that you may be perfect and complete, lacking nothing" (1:2–4).

Do you want the peaceable fruit of righteousness? You can have it. Respond properly to the chastening of God in your life. Do you want to be mature, lacking in nothing? You can be. Respond properly to the trials that will come into your life.

The process of growing into Christlikeness requires five ingredients: the work of God, the word of God, personal commitment, other believers, and time and trials.

Why Don't We Change More Quickly and More Completely?

We don't change more quickly and more completely because God has decreed that we be transformed over time and because of the complications of sin.

Central Passage: 1 Peter 2:2, *As newborn babes, desire the pure milk of the word, that you may grow thereby.*

We have made several allusions to this question, but it will be helpful to stop and talk about it. We all wish we were farther down the road spiritually than we are. Why don't we change more quickly, and why isn't our change more all-encompassing? Why do I change in one area and not another? The bottom line is, "I don't know." But let's speculate together for a moment. There are three things to consider.

God Is a Picturing God

All spiritual truth is pictured by something physical. Death and resurrection, for example, are pictured by the seasons. In fall, the earth begins to die until, by winter, it is dead. In spring, new life begins to stir, and in summer the resurrection of the globe is complete. In another example, the Old Testament sacrificial system is a picture of the spiritual atonement that Jesus accomplished for us. Again, marriage is a picture of the relationship that Christians will have with Jesus in heaven. God is a picturing God.

God has given us a picture in the process of human physical life. A person is born a helpless infant, totally dependent on others for his needs. Through proper care and nourishment, he begins to grow physically and mentally. The person progresses from infancy to childhood to youth to adulthood. The same thing happens spiritually. When someone becomes a Christian, the Bible says he is "born again" (John 3:7). As a new child, he must drink spiritual milk, continue to grow, and pro-gress to the point at which he can eat spiritual solid food (Hebrews 5:12–14).

A physical child can see adults and want to be like them. So can a spiritual child. A physical child stretches, fails, tries again, fails, and tries again. So does a spiritual child. When I was a child, basketball was my passion. My older brother was a good player, and I was consumed by a desire to be like him. I used to jump and jump around the house. When I was ten or twelve, I would try to jump and touch the kitchen ceiling. When I could touch it, I then wanted to be able to hit it with the palm of my hand. Then, my goal was to get my elbow that high, and, finally, my head. I was a compulsive jumper, never satisfied with how high I could jump or how tall I was. My mother is a saint for having put up with me (though she once made me wash the dirty finger streaks off the kitchen ceiling).

God intended us to "grow," not "poof" into maturity. The fact that we grow slowly physically and want to be more than we are and do more than we can physically is merely a picture of the same spiritual truth.

Limitations

When I was growing up, I had injuries, illness, and other inherent limitations. I had ankle and knee injuries that limited my potential. I never got as tall as I wanted to be and never jumped as high as I wanted to jump. Why? Because I was limited by the genes I inherited, and because the Fall of humanity resulted in things like disease and accidents. Some of my accidents have left permanent limitations. The same is true spiritually. The Fall results in our being susceptible to spiritual disease and accidents, and we have inherent limitations. I cannot be the second Billy Graham. I am not gifted or called to be. I have permanent spiritual scars from things in my past. I have permanent spiritual weaknesses. I may be strong where you are weak. I may be weak where you are strong. That is simply the way it is. Because of God's plan to have us "grow" rather than "poof" into maturity, and because of the effects of the Fall and sin in our lives, we will never be all that we want to be on this side of heaven

The Grace of God

Despite our limitations, God's grace covers all our sins. God's love overcomes all our shortcomings. God "knows our frame; He is mindful that we are but dust" (Psalm 103:14, NASB). Plus, God is not finished with us yet. We are not yet what we are going to be. He will ultimately perfect us in every regard when we join Him in heaven. Until then, we must be satisfied with the fact that, in the eyes of God, because of Jesus, we are perfect.

Speed Bump!

Slow down to be sure you've gotten the main points of this chapter.

Question
Answer

Q1. What is the goal of spiritual change?

A1. The goal of spiritual change is *transformation* into the spiritual likeness of Jesus.

Q2. What is at the heart of spiritual change?

A2. At the heart of spiritual change is an *interaction* in which the Holy Spirit prompts and the individual responds.

Q3. What process must we go through to become like Christ?

A3. To become like Christ requires the *combination* of the work of God, the word of God, personal commitment, other believers, and time and trials.

Q4. Why don't we change more quickly and more completely?

A4. We don't change more quickly and more completely because God has decreed that we be transformed over *time* and because of the complications of sin.

Fill in the Blank

Question **A**nswer

Q1. What is the goal of spiritual change?

A1. The goal of spiritual change is _____ into the spiritual likeness of Jesus.

Q2. What is at the heart of spiritual change?

A2. At the heart of spiritual change is an _____ in which the Holy Spirit prompts and the individual responds.

Q3. What process must we go through to become like Christ?

A3. To become like Christ requires the _____ of the work of God, the word of God, personal commitment, other believers, and time and trials.

Q4. Why don't we change more quickly and more completely?

A4. We don't change more quickly and more completely because God has decreed that we be transformed over _____ and because of the complications of sin.

For Further Thought and Discussion

1. If spiritual likeness to Christ is the goal of the work of the Holy Spirit in your life, what are the strong areas and the weak areas of your character?

2. In the interaction process between the Holy Spirit and the individual, do you tend to rely more on human effort or on God "moving" you? Or do you tend to neglect the process?

3. In what area of the process toward spiritual maturity are you doing best? In what area (work of God, word of God, personal commitment, other believers, time and trials) are you doing worst?

4. Are you satisfied with how quickly you are changing for the better? What do you think is the single greatest reason you do not change more quickly?

What If I Don't Believe?

If I don't believe in the process the Holy Spirit uses to change me into the spiritual image of Christ, then:

1. I may be very frustrated with the things in my life that I don't want, or frustrated with the absence of things that I want, because I don't realize that these things can be used by God to make me more like Christ.

2. I may not participate in the process in a helpful way, and thereby slow my spiritual growth and stunt my potential.

3. I may lack patience, not realizing that growth over time is inevitable, and I will never "poof" my way to maturity.

For Further Study

1. Scripture
Several passages speak to how the Holy Spirit changes us. They include:

- John 15:5
- Romans 6:1–14
- Romans 7:18–25
- Romans 12:1–2
- Galatians 5:22–23

- Ephesians 2:8–9

- Philippians 2:12–13

- Hebrews 5:12–14

2. Books
Several other books are very helpful in studying this subject. They are listed below in general order of difficulty. If I could read only one of these, I would read the first one.

Flying Closer to the Flame, Charles Swindoll
Keep in Step with the Spirit, James I. Packer
I Believe in the Holy Spirit, Michael Green

*If we prune back that part of our activity
which is not really fruitful in the Holy Spirit,
we find that we do less, but accomplish more.*
■ John Michael Talbot

How Does the Holy Spirit Use Me?

I love dogs. I always have. When I was a child, I checked out library books with pictures of all the different breeds of dogs and information on their background and characteristics. I used to dream about what kind of dog I would most like to have. I finally narrowed the list down to six and decided I might need a small kennel to be happy. Well, I'm an adult now, I don't have even one dog, and I am happy anyway. But I still like dogs.

I continue to be amazed at how different dogs can be. Take hunting dogs, for instance. Three hundred and sixty days of the year, they are normal dogs. But on the days they are actually taken hunting, they are transformed into something quite different from a mere household pet. If the master walks out of the house with a shotgun in his hand, something clicks in the dog's mind, and it switches from being Dr. Jekyll to become Mr. Hyde. Sometimes the dog will shadow the master, waiting for the magic moment when he heads for the pickup truck. Then the grand moment comes. The tailgate of the pickup drops and the dog flies into the back. It begins to shiver and whine in anticipation, looking more like it is freezing and starving to death than merely anticipating the hunt. There is a tense, nervous, almost painful look on its face. When the truck gets to the field where they are to hunt for quail or pheasant, the tailgate drops down, and the dog takes off running frantically, zigzagging back and forth across the meadow hunting for birds. The dog may give out an occasional yip, yip, yip as it is running. Then if it hits a scent, the yip turns to a yeeoow, yeeoow, yeeoow. It sometimes sounds as if it has been injured. But it is sheer ecstasy. Finally, if it hits a hot scent, the yeeoow turns into a berserk roooo-roooo-roooo-roooo-roooo!

This whole scenario changes, of course, depending on the kind of dog, what it is hunting, and how it has been trained. But one thing is certain: Hunting dogs love to hunt more than anything.

Compare that with an Alaskan sled dog. I remember watching a "special" on television about the Iditarod Trail Sled Dog Race held each year in Alaska, a grueling race covering many miles of frozen wasteland in almost intolerable winter conditions. The documentary showed how the dogs were bred, selected, and trained for the race. Then, it showed the race. There are teams of about eight or nine dogs who, at night, lie like furry donuts in the snow, often buried by the snow while sleeping. A little "chimney" in the snow, melted out by the dog's breath, is all that can be seen, with little puffs of steam rising up through the hole in the snow each time the dog exhales. But when the driver appears, the snow-covered donuts explode into barking, yelping, jumping units of inexhaustible energy. When the driver mounts the sled and yells "Mush!" the dogs strain eagerly against their harnesses, trying desperately to get the sled up to speed. Their eyes are wide with excitement, and their tongues loll out of the sides of their mouths in undisguised pleasure. In an interview, the trainer said, "The dogs are only completely happy when they are on the trail."

In this chapter we learn that . . .

1. A spiritual gift is a God-given ability for ministry to others.
2. Office gifts are given to those who serve the church at large in a specific capacity: apostle, prophet, evangelist, and pastor-teacher.
3. Service gifts are nonmiraculous gifts that correspond to ministries that all of us should do, but some individuals are gifted for greater impact in those ministries.
4. Special gifts are miraculous or supernormal gifts that appear to be given for the purpose not only of meeting a need of the moment but also for validating the message of Christianity to those who have not heard or believed.

Now think about what would happen if you were to switch the dogs. Suppose you put the huge Alaskan husky in the back of a pickup and took him out to a grassy field full of pheasant and quail. It would jump down from the back of the truck and say in its little doggy mind, "What's this? Where's the snow? Where are the trails? Where's the sled, the harness, the other dogs? This place is the pits. There's nothing here." A bird could flush right in front of its nose, and it would create an annoyance rather than excitement. This huge, big-boned, thick-furred running machine would be lost and bewildered.

It would be even worse for a short-haired pointer to be put in a sled team in Alaska. Its would say in *its* little doggy mind, "What is this?!? I'm fu-reeeezing! And what's this leather harness? It's like a strait jacket. And what's worse, you can't smell a thing through all this snow. There could be a million quail around here, and no dog would ever know it for all the snow." This small, quick, smelling machine would be equally lost and bewildered.

Each of the dogs is gifted to do something special, but it is quite out of place in a vastly different environment.

The same is true of people. Someone once said that if George Washington had tried to be an inventor, and Benjamin Franklin had tried to be a military man, we would probably be sitting in the dark today, talking with a British accent.

Why I need to know this

I need to know that I have a spiritual gift, or I may not only fail to serve the Lord as effectively as I might but also to enjoy my service to Him as fully as He wants me to. There are some gifts I will never have, but all Christians need each other as we live in a context of mutual ministry.

It is no secret that all of us are good at some things and not so good at other things. One of the great tricks in life is to get ourselves fitted into the right slot—a round peg in a round hole or a square peg in a square hole, and not the other way around. We have different levels of intelligence, different kinds of intelligence, different aptitudes, different talents, different temperaments, and different interests. All these make us different kinds of people with different contributions to make to the world.

What Is a Spiritual Gift?

A spiritual gift is a God-given ability for ministry to others.

Central Passage: 1 Peter 4:10, *As each one has received a gift, minister it to one another, as good stewards of the manifold grace of God.*

Not only do we differ in natural gifts and abilities, but the Bible teaches us that each Christian also has been given a spiritual gift, or possibly several spiritual gifts. Only Christians have spiritual gifts, because the Holy Spirit gives these gifts and only does so after He comes to dwell within the believer (1 Corinthians 12:11). These are not just finely honed natural abilities; they are special God-given abilities to minister to others. Sometimes they correspond closely with our natural talents, but they are more than just talents.

The Bible has much to say about spiritual gifts, but there are many different interpretations of the information. In researching for this chapter, I have read several books, consulted a number of others, and received a summary of research from a rather large selection of books on the Holy Spirit. It is safe to say that no two of the books agree on all things. The best we can say is that people tend to fall into one of several "camps." One camp generally believes that "miraculous" spiritual gifts still exist as they did in the Bible, and the other camp generally doesn't.

I cannot offer a definitive treatment of spiritual gifts that will answer all the questions. There are some clear areas of agreement, however, and we should look at those before we look at the areas where perspectives differ.

> Each Christian has a gift from the Holy Spirit.

First, each Christian has a spiritual gift. First Peter 4:10 says, "each one." Paul writes in 1 Corinthians 12:7, "each one." Romans 12:3 says "each one." Each one of us has a spiritual gift.

Second, the gifts are to be used in love. First Peter 4:8 says we are to "have fervent love for one another," as we minister our gift to others (4:10). Romans 12:10 says that we must be "kindly affectionate to one another with brotherly love, in honor giving preference for one another," as we use our spiritual gifts (Romans 12:4–6). First Corinthians 12:7 teaches that the use of our spiritual gifts must be "for the profit of all."

Third, the gifts are for the benefit of one another, as has already been stated or implied. First Peter 4:10 says, "Minister . . . to *one another*." Romans 12:5 says, "We, being many, are one body in Christ, and individually members of *one another*," and therefore, minister to one another. Ephesians 4:12 says that our gifts are "for the equipping of the saints for the work of ministry, for the edifying of the body of Christ." (Italics added.)

We see, then, that the spiritual gifts that we all have are not for the purpose of building up or advancing ourselves, but for serving one another in love. We are to use our spiritual gift; it is an obligation.

In talking about spiritual gifts, I have chosen three terms

that are not in the Bible, but which I have found helpful in understanding spiritual gifts. Those terms are "office gifts," "service gifts," and "special gifts." A person, for example, with the office gift of pastor-teacher might have the service gift of teaching.

What Are the Office Gifts?

Office gifts are given to those who serve the church at large in a specific capacity: apostle, prophet, evangelist, and pastor-teacher.

Central Passage: Ephesians 4:11–12, *And He Himself gave some to be apostles, some prophets, some evangelists, and some pastors and teachers, for the equipping of the saints for the work of ministry, for the edifying of the body of Christ.*

There are three primary categories of spiritual gifts in the New Testament, each one called by a different name. The office gifts are introduced by the Greek word *domata*. It refers to individuals who are gifted and called by God to play the determinative role in establishing, increasing, and overseeing the church. The first two offices, apostles and prophets, seem to have been foundational gifts of the early church that, many believe, disappeared after the church was established. Ephesians 2:20 says that the household of God, the church, was "built on the foundation of the apostles and prophets, Jesus Christ Himself being the chief cornerstone."

Ephesians 2:21–22 goes on to say, "in whom [Jesus] the whole building [the church], being fitted together, grows into a holy temple in the Lord, in whom you also are being built together for a dwelling place of God in the Spirit." This means that after the cornerstone was laid (Jesus' teachings, life, death, resurrection, and ascension), then the rest of the foundation was laid by the apostles and prophets. Then, the rest of history, from then until the present day, sees a great superstructure being added, and that superstructure is the totality of all Christians from the time of Christ's first coming until He comes again.

The gifted individuals who are called by God to oversee the building of that superstructure are evangelists and pastor-teachers. These, then, are the office gifts. The first two seem to have been temporary, and the last two seem to be permanent.

An alternative view sees Jesus to be the keystone, as the critical last stone that holds the stones of an arch in place, or the "head of the corner" (Psalm 118:22), the stone placed at the top of the struc-ture to tie two walls together at the corner. Between the founda-tion of the apostles and prophets of the earliest church and the exalted Lord as the keystone, the church grows up unto Christ. The image brings together a literal temple building with that of a living being that continues to grow, with Christ as the ex-alted Head.

Among those who hold this view are many Pentecostal, charismatic, and "third wave" Christians, whose views are explained more fully in the next chapter. These believe that all New Testament gifts continue to operate in the church until Christ's return, including the ministries, or the offices, of apostle and prophet. They agree, however, that first-generation apostles were unique in their direct commissioning from the risen Lord and in their authority to define and establish the gospel and doctrine for the church for all time. Their unique authority had two important results: (1) making clear that the gospel was not just for Jews, but for all who believed in Christ; and (2) the writing of New Testa-ment Scripture. Apart from this important uniqueness, those who believe that all gifts remain in effect until Christ's return believe that modern-day apostles are those God uses to extend the work of the church remarkably, opening fields to the gospel and over-seeing larger sections of the body of Christ.

What Are the Service Gifts?

Service gifts are nonmiraculous gifts that correspond to ministries that all of us should do, but some individuals are gifted for greater impact in those ministries.

Central Passage: Romans 12:6–8, *Having then gifts differing according to the grace that is given to us, let us use them: if prophecy, let us prophesy in proportion to our faith; or ministry, let us use it in our ministering; he who teaches, in teaching; he who exhorts, in exhortation; he who gives, with liberality; he who leads, with diligence; he who shows mercy, with cheerfulness.*

A second kind of spiritual gift is introduced in the New Testament by the Greek word *charismaton*. While there are nonmiraculous gifts mentioned in 1 Corinthians 12, the third major passage discussing spiritual gifts, the Romans 12 passage remains the central passage for nonmiraculous gifts. "Prophecy" in Romans 12, for reasons that I will go into later, probably does not mean the ability to predict the future, but rather the powerful proclamation of the word of God. In addition to prophecy, we see the service gifts of ministering (serving or helping), teaching, exhorting, giving, leading, and mercy. There is no biblical definition of these gifts, but general definitions of the gifts seem rather self-evident:

1. Prophecy: the supernatural ability to proclaim the word of God to others.
2. Helping: the supernatural ability to serve, support, and sustain others in need.
3. Teaching: the supernatural ability to help others understand the truths of the word of God.
4. Exhorting: the supernatural ability to encourage and challenge others.
5. Giving: the supernatural ability to meet the physical (mainly financial) needs of others.
6. Leading: the supernatural ability to motivate others to pursue a worthy goal.
7. Mercy: the supernatural ability to show love and compassion to others.

Few question that these gifts are in force today. A few debate it, but only a few. Most agree that these service gifts are alive and well in the church. While only certain people are gifted by God in these areas (one person might have the gifts of mercy and giving, another person might have the gift of teaching, etc.), all of us are responsible to function in these areas.

Spiritual gift	Command to all
Helping:	"In everything I showed you that by working hard in this manner you must help the weak." Acts 20:35 (NASB)
Teaching:	"Go therefore . . . teaching them to observe all things that I have commanded you." Matthew 28:19–20
Exhortation:	"Not forsaking our own assembling together, . . . but encouraging one another." Hebrews 10:25 (NASB)

Giving:	"Let each one give as he purposes in his heart, not grudgingly or of necessity; for God loves a cheerful giver." 2 Corinthians 9:7
Leading:	"You also became imitators of us and of the Lord, having received the word in much tribulation with the joy of the Holy Spirit, so that you became an example to all the believers in Macedonia and in Achaia." 1 Thessalonians 1:6–7 (NASB)
Mercy:	"Blessed are the merciful, for they shall obtain mercy." Matthew 5:7

What Are Special Gifts?

Special gifts are miraculous or supernormal gifts that appear to be given for the purpose not only of meeting a need of the moment but also for validating the message of Christianity to those who have not heard or believed.

Central Passage: 1 Corinthians 12:7–11, *But the manifestation of the Spirit is given to each one for the profit of all: for to one is given the word of wisdom through the Spirit, to another the word of knowledge through the same Spirit, to another faith by the same Spirit, to another gifts of healings by the same Spirit, to another the working of miracles, to another prophecy, to another discerning of spirits, to another different kinds of tongues, to another the interpretation of tongues. But one and the same Spirit works all these things, distributing to each one individually as He wills.*

The third category of gifts is introduced by the Greek word *phanerosis*, which means a "manifestation" (1 Corinthians 12:7). These gifts are supernatural, above and beyond any normal ability. Healing people, speaking in unknown tongues, interpreting what was said in the unknown tongue, performing miracles—all would have to be considered beyond the normal daily routine for most people. Again, no biblical definitions exist, but we can take an educated guess at what they mean:

1. *Word of wisdom:* the supernatural ability to discern the wisdom of God for a given situation.

2. *Word of knowledge:* the supernatural ability to knowsomething that is true, such as something that may happen in the future.

3. *Faith:* the supernatural ability to exercise great faith in a situation.

4. *Healing:* the supernatural ability to heal people of physical maladies.

5. *Miracles:* the supernatural ability to perform various miracles.

6. *Prophecy:* the supernatural ability to proclaim the word of God with power and to predict the future.

7. *Discerning of spirits:* the supernatural ability to determine the presence or influence of evil spirits.

8. *Tongues:* the supernatural ability to speak in unknown languages.

9. *Interpretation:* the supernatural ability to give the meaning of an utterance of an unknown tongue.

The exercise of these gifts often met the immediate needs of those with physical maladies or other pressing needs. In other cases, the exercise of these gifts is said to build up Christians (1 Corinthians 14:4–5, 22); yet in Hebrews 2:4, they are said to have been for the purpose of validating the new message of salvation by grace through faith in Jesus.

As we will see later, Christians differ as to whether or not God intends these special gifts to operate today. Pentecostal, charismatic, and "third wave" Christians believe that these gifts were given to the church until Christ returns. They would also emphasize that these gifts are themselves dimensions of the gospel of Christ expressed in deeds and not just signs that point to a gospel that is separate from the deeds themselves. For example, God's gift of healing a sick person (whether by the earthly Jesus or by the ascended Jesus who heals now through His church) comes not merely to validate or prove the truth that believers are saved by God's grace through faith in Jesus. Instead, such a gift actually demonstrates God's saving grace (the healing is a grace-gift) and is itself one dimension of the salvation set in process by Jesus in His earthly ministry. This process continues through His church until His return, when the many dimensions of salvation are complete and all pain, sorrow, crying, and death pass away

(Revelation 21:3–5). This view is discussed more fully in the next chapter.

Conclusion

This is probably the place to note that no list of spiritual gifts in the Bible is the same. Rather than a fixed, exclusive list of gifts with technical definitions, it seems we have been given a representative list of gifts. Common sense will indicate how the gifts are to function. If our list is representative, then it is possible that other gifts exist. For example, some people have a remarkable gift for hospitality; their homes are always open to people for ministry of one kind or another. And, in the New Testament, we are encouraged to be hospitable. If someone said he thought he had the gift of hospitality, I would not quarrel with that possibility from what I understand of Scripture.

In addition, we are never *commanded* to know our gift. Concerning the office gifts, the gift of an evangelist or pastor-teacher will eventually become apparent. Those who evangelize or shepherd and teach with an inner compulsion (in the right sense of the word) will see results that are not experienced by those who do not have such a gift.

Our gifts become apparent as we use them.

We are all instructed to do all the things in the list of service gifts. As we do all those things, experience will reveal what our gift is. Our gift is usually the thing that we see the most clearly, have the greatest burden for, enjoy doing most, and in which we see the most results.

Concerning the special gifts, 1 Corinthians 12:11 says that the Spirit distributes these individually as He wills, and they are so out of the ordinary that if someone had a special gift, it would be clear to all.

The Bible talks much more about our responsibility to live in love and compassion toward others than about focusing on our gifts. As we try to manifest the character of Christ and proclaim His name to others, our gift usually will become apparent. Even if it doesn't, that is no major problem. However, it can be helpful to study the spiritual gifts and get guidance if it is available, to help assess what our gift might be. That way, we might be spared the trauma of trying to function in an area in which we are not gifted or may even be weak.

Speed Bump!

Slow down to be sure you've gotten the main points of this chapter.

$\mathcal{Q}$uestion   **Q1.** What is a spiritual gift?

$\mathcal{A}$nswer   **A1.** A spiritual gift is a God-given *ability* for ministry to others.

Q2. What are the office gifts?

A2. Office gifts are given to those who serve the church at large in a *specific* capacity: apostle, prophet, evangelist, and pastor-teacher.

Q3. What are the service gifts?

A3. Service gifts are *nonmiraculous* gifts that correspond to ministries that all of us should do, but some individuals are gifted for greater impact in those ministries.

Q4. What are special gifts?

A4. Special gifts are *miraculous* or supernormal gifts that appear to be given for the purpose not only of meeting a need of the moment but also for validating the message of Christianity to those who have not heard or believed.

Fill in the Blanks

$\mathcal{Q}$uestion   **Q1.** What is a spiritual gift?

$\mathcal{A}$nswer   **A1.** A spiritual gift is a God-given _____ for ministry to others.

Q2. What are the office gifts?

A2. Office gifts are given to those who serve the church at large in a _____ capacity: apostle, prophet, evangelist, and pastor-teacher.

Q3. What are the service gifts?

A3. Service gifts are _____ gifts that correspond to ministries that all of us should do, but some individuals are gifted for greater impact in those areas.

Q4. What are the special gifts?

A4. Special gifts are _____ or supernormal gifts that appear to be given for the purpose not only of meeting a need of the moment but also for validating the message of Christianity to those who have not heard or believed.

For Further Thought and Discussion

1. Based on what you see as important, on what you enjoy doing, and on what you seem to have success at, what spiritual gift or gifts do you think you may possess? Have others affirmed your conclusions?

2. How do you think someone could express the gift of pastor-teacher if he were not vocationally employed by a local church? What are some ways a church member might express a gift of evangelism?

3. If we are all to serve in all areas of service gifts, what do you see as a potential spiritual gift in this area? In what area do you see yourself as being weakest?

What If I Don't Believe?

If I do not believe in spiritual gifts, I may miss out on a rich experience of serving the Lord in a meaningful way. I also may get stuck "being faithful" doing something at which I am not effective, when someone else could do it much better. I may fall into the trap of thinking I should do too much, or the opposite, of thinking I should do too little. If I do not understand the difference between miraculous and nonmiraculous gifts, I may think there is something wrong with me if I do not experience a miraculous gift.

For Further Study

1. Scripture

- Romans 12:3–8
- 1 Corinthians 12:4–11, 28–31
- Ephesians 2:19–22
- Ephesians 4:11–16

2. Books

Several other books are very helpful in studying this subject. They are listed below in general order of difficulty. If I could read only one of these, I would read the first one.

The Holy Spirit, Billy Graham
Keep in Step with the Spirit, James I. Packer
I Believe in the Holy Spirit, Michael Green

*Perception of ideas rather than the storing of
them should be the aim of education. The
mind should be an eye to see with rather than
a bin to store facts in. The man who has been
taught by the Holy Spirit will be a seer rather
than a scholar. The difference is that the
scholar sees and the seer sees through; and
that is a mighty difference indeed.*
■ A.W. Tozer (1897–1963)

Are Signs and Wonders Valid for Today?

Attorney Carl Black recalls a trial in which an eminent psychologist was called to testify. A severe, no-nonsense professional, she sat down in the witness chair, unaware that its rear legs were set precariously near the back of the raised platform.

"Will you state your name?" asked the district attorney.

Tilting back in her chair, she opened her mouth to answer, but instead catapulted head over heels backward and landed in a stack of exhibits and recording equipment. Everyone watched in stunned silence as she extricated herself, rearranged her disheveled dress and hair, and was reseated on the witness stand. The glare she directed at onlookers dared anyone to so much as smirk.

"Well, doctor," continued the district attorney without changing expression, "we could start with an easier question." (*Reader's Digest* [August 1993], 109)

When someone asks the question, "Are signs and wonders valid for today?" we mentally catapult head over heels and land in a stack of assumptions and contradictory information. Then we get up, all disheveled, wondering if we could start with an easier question. But this question has to be looked at. And no matter what answer you give, not everyone is going to agree.

There are at least three major positions on this question, and in the interest of advancing maximum understanding among Christians, I want to briefly describe each one. There will be those who feel that I have not done justice to their positions, but these brief comments will be representative of many within these "camps."

What Is the Durative Position?

The Durative position is the belief that the signs and wonders in the New Testament have continued throughout church history and still exist today.

This is the position held by a large percentage of Pentecostal, charismatic, and third wave believers. Before we look more closely at the position, however, it might be helpful to understand these twentieth-century terms better. The first wave of signs and wonders came in the Pentecostal movement in the first part of this century, beginning in the United States and spreading to other parts of the world. It emphasized the experience of being baptized in the Holy Spirit, accompanied by speaking in tongues. Signs and wonders were seen to naturally accompany preaching and belief in this full experience of the gospel. Because Pentecostalism was largely rejected by the established churches, Pentecostal believers organized their own churches. Most of the supernormal activity of the first wave thus took place within Pentecostal churches or circles.

The second wave came in the charismatic renewal of the middle part of the century. Unlike the first wave, the charismatic movement spilled over into the major denominations, including the Catholic Church. This wave too focused on the baptism of the Holy Spirit, which again usually included speaking in tongues. Charismatics emphasized "all" the gifts of the Spirit operating and getting everyone functioning in the body of Christ according to his or her gift. The term "charismatic" was taken from the Greek word for gifts, *charismata*. Charismatics also emphasized exuberant worship, compassion for those in need, and warm, interpersonal relationships—things that many felt often to be missing in noncharismatic circles.

The third wave is a more recent phenomenon, beginning in the 1980's. While third wave believers applaud the work of the Holy Spirit they see in the first two waves, they choose not to be identified with either. Third wave renewal emphasizes miracles, physical healing, demonic exorcisms, and emotional healing. It tends to hold to the classic evangelical view that baptism in the Spirit occurs at conversion and to a role for speaking in tongues that is relatively minor, compared to the first two waves. Many third wavers prefer a less enthusiastic form of worship and are frequently content in traditional evangelical worship services.

Pentecostals, charismatics, and third wave believers generally hold to a Durative perspective on sign gifts. They believe the miraculous spiritual gifts and the signs and wonders that occurred in the New Testament still occur today, as they have to one degree or another since New Testament times. For this reason, we will, for our purposes, lump the varied Pentecostal, charismatic, and third wave positions under the umbrella of the "signs and wonders movement."

In this chapter we learn that . . .

1. The Durative position is the belief that the signs and wonders in the New Testament have continued throughout church history and still exist today.
2. The Cessationist position states that New Testament signs and wonders disappeared with the passing of the apostles and the establishment of the Scriptures and are not intended ever to reappear again.
3. The Approximation position holds that the miraculous gifts and signs and wonders are not fully operative today, but that a reduced form of the gifts operates today under the apparent blessing of God.

These signs and wonders, according to this position, include the following common manifestations of the Spirit:

Tongues: Modern tongues include the miraculous, but infrequent, speaking of an unknown foreign language so that the hearer hears God praised in his or her own language, as we see happening in the second chapter of the book of Acts. More commonly, tongues occur as the speaking of an unknown prayer language that is either to be spoken in private or, if in public, be interpreted by someone with the gift of interpretation, as we see in 1 Corinthians 14.

Interpretation: This gift enables one to interpret the foreign or unknown language that someone else is speaking. It is not understood to be a close, word-for-word translation, but an adequate interpretation of the tongue uttered.

Healings: This gift is the actual healing of physical disease, illness, or malady. Some view the gift also as in some sense residing with persons given this gift, with the result that when they pray in faith, those afflicted are frequently healed by God (never by the person with the gift).

Prophecy: This gift refers to a divinely inspired proclamation of God's will, usually for a specific situation. It may but does not have to include the element of prediction, and it is never viewed as having the authority to supplant or override God's written word.

Exorcism: This gift consists both of the Spirit-given ability to discern the influence of demonic spirits and to effectively command them to leave individuals under their influence.

Evaluation

Some, of course, see major problems with this position. Among them are (1) the biblical violations and excesses of the signs and wonders movement; (2) the fact that, to many, the gifts in the New Testament seem much more predictable, effective, dramatic, and verifiable than today; and (3) biblical and historical support for the view that the signs and wonders recorded in the New Testament may have existed for a specific purpose, and when that purpose passed, the signs and wonders themselves passed.

What Is the Cessationist Position?

The Cessationist position states that New Testament signs and wonders disappeared with the passing of the apostles and the establishment of the Scriptures and are not intended ever to reappear again.

The Cessationist position, generally, holds the following views:

Tongues: Modern tongues are a psychological phenomenon at best and demonic at worst. Glossolalia (speaking in tongues) is not confined to Pentecostal, charismatic, or third wave movements. It is found among Eskimos, Eastern religions, New Agers, those in mental institutions, and occultists. This is not to say that Christians fall into any of these categories. It is merely to say that tongues by themselves are not a sign of anything. Apparently, a certain percentage of people have the innate capacity to speak in tongues, and some do so in Christian contexts. It does not, however, constitute a duplication of the New Testament gift.

Interpretations: Since biblical tongues do not exist, there is no need for the gift of interpretation either.

Healings: God does heal miraculously today. However, the healings that are seen in charismatic circles today occur in answer to prayer, by God's sovereign decision to heal, or as a result of powerful psychological forces that can affect healing. The New Testament gift of healing does not exist.

Prophecy: The ability to tell the future or to speak directly for God is a gift that passed with the apostles and New Testament prophets and does not exist today.

Exorcisms: No gift of discerning spirits or exorcism exists today. The epistles tell us to have our spiritual armor in place and stand firm (Ephesians 6:10–18), and to resist the devil and he will flee from us (James 4:7).

Evaluation

There are problems with a rigid Cessationist position also. First, nowhere in the Bible are signs and wonders and miraculous gifts of the Spirit explicitly said to have ceased, never to reappear again. Add to that the fact that many bright young Pentecostal, charismatic, and third wave scholars are amassing better biblical support for the validity of their positions—and answering objections to their position—than they have ever done before. Their diligent scholarship has made the standard Cessationist argu-

---

Why I need to know if signs and wonders are valid today:

Unless I understand what the Bible teaches about signs and wonders, I may fall prey to an illicit use of them, or, on the other hand, I may discount something that is actually a work of God. I neither want to be deluded into believing in something that is not of God, nor to miss out on what God is doing in His world.

---

ments more vulnerable. In addition, strict Cessationists who allow for little or no miraculous activity today must find a way to explain many rather amazing things that are reported by sound, mature Christians.

For example, I have friends ministering in primitive areas who tell stories of unbelievable things. These are people whom I respect in every other way, but they have these outrageous stories to tell, often relating to demonic activity.

My wife and I also have a close friend who is a woman of unusual wisdom, maturity, and insight. She has sacrificed most modern comforts for a life of hardship and deprivation as a missionary. Yet she is only really happy when she is on the mission field. She is a lady of grace, humility, and solid biblical knowledge. She is not a Pentecostal or a charismatic, and she has nothing in her past to predispose her toward anything sensational. Yet when she talks of what has happened to her, to Christian friends of hers, or to other people she knows, your jaw goes slack and the hair at the back of your neck prickles. She tells stories of what could be called "power encounters" and "power evangelism," because there are signs and wonders that surround her life and ministry.

We have another friend from Africa whose preaching ministry in his home country has been accompanied by astonishing manifestations of the power of God, especially in areas of high demonic activity, though he himself is not Pentecostal, charismatic, or third wave.

It is common to hear reports from missionaries and read stories of missionaries in primitive parts of Africa, Asia, the Philippines, and other places, telling stories of visible angels surrounding and protecting missionary housing, of Elijah-like fire erupting spontaneously on ceremonial altars to prove which god was the true God, or of miraculous healings. The people who tell these stories are bright people, people of integrity, people of biblical knowledge and spiritual maturity. They are people who appear normal in every respect except one: Their lives are interwoven with miraculous events.

Similar stories increasingly are being told by people in inner city ghettos, in wealthy suburbs where Satan worship and the occult are growing at an alarming rate, and in more modern countries (as opposed to Third World countries), such as Russia and China, where Christianity had been "officially" stamped out.

What do you do with such people? You can look them squarely in the eyes and call them bold-faced liars. You can listen politely, and then afterwards tell your spouse what a pity it is that they have one corner flapping in the wind. You can believe they are deluded, tricked, or having regular bad dreams. Or you can accept what they are saying as true, and then go back to the Bible to see if you can "square" it with Scripture. Non-Pentecostal/charismatics/third wavers do so, sometimes, by advancing what some have called an "Approximation" position.

What Is the Approximation Position?

The Approximation position holds that the miraculous gifts and signs and wonders are not fully operative today, but that a reduced form of the gifts operates today under the apparent blessing of God.

The "Durative" view and the "Cessationist" view both can be presented rather easily because they paint the issues in black and white. One says that the full New Testament miraculous gifts and signs and wonders are in existence today, and the other says they aren't. Positions other than these two usually take careful, more thorough explanation. While variations of this position are espoused by many, one version has been well articulated by James Packer in his book *Keep in Step with the Spirit* (especially chapter 6).

He makes the point that if you apply two key biblical criteria to the modern signs and wonders movement, you have a measure of its validity. First is a doctrinal test: "Do they declare that Jesus is Lord?" (1 John 2:22; 4:1–3). Second is a moral test: "Do they manifest love for God by keeping His commandments, striving to avoid sin and loving their brethren in Christ?" (1 John 2:4; 3:9–10, 17, 24; 4:7–13, 20–21; 5:1–3). By these two tests, he asserts, the modern charismatic movement, as a whole, passes the tests (Packer 185).

He goes on to state that "most Protestant charismatics outside Germany embrace . . . the restorationist view," making the essence of the disciples' experience on the Day of Pentecost, as described in Acts 2, and of the Corinthians' experience, as described in 1 Corinthians 12–14, into norms, ideals, and goals for Christians now. (The difference between the Durative view [my term] and the Restorationist view [Packer's term] is that the Durative view holds that the gifts never disappeared. The Restorationist view holds that they did disappear in the centuries following Christ, but have been restored today.)

In what he calls a "retheologized view," Packer argues that the miraculous gifts and the signs and wonders of the New Testament are not convincingly in operation today, but that an approximation of the gifts is, with God's apparent blessing—hence the name "Approximation" view. This view, as explained by Packer, holds these positions on the following issues:

Tongues: Modern tongues are not the supernatural ability to speak foreign languages as they were in the Bible, but are essentially a spiritual/psychological phenomenon that, like any meaningful spiritual experience, may help a person live a more satisfying and fruitful life. Charismatic glossolalia (speaking in tongues), which is frequently a learned skill and technique, lacks language structure, and its own practitioners regard it as mainly for private use. It cannot be convincingly equated with the tongues of 1 Corinthians 12–14, which were for public use, served as a sign to unbelievers, and which Paul apparently considered a language conveying meaning and therefore capable of being interpreted. Even though it is not a restoration of a New Testament gift, God is using glossolalia today to enrich people's personal spiritual lives. It is subject to misuse and disappointment for some, but that does not discount its positive benefit to others if we are to take abundant personal testimony at face value.

Interpretation: If modern tongues are not a restoration of the New Testament gift, then modern interpretation is the least credible of all modern charismatic manifestations. Packer suggests that "interpretations prove to be as stereotyped, vague, and uninformative as they are spontaneous, fluent, and confident."

Healings: Jesus and the apostles healed directly with their word or their touch, healing was instantaneous, and they healed in very large numbers. On occasion they raised individuals who had been dead for days. There is no record that they ever attempted to heal without success (except in the one case of demon possession where the disciples failed to pray and Jesus had to take over [Mark 9:17–29]), and no one who was healed relapsed soon after. Whatever else can be said of modern faith healers, none of them has a track record like this.

> **Healing in the New Testament was successful, instantaneous, and permanent.**

Several things must be said under "healings," however. First, it must be admitted that God does appear to be healing miraculously today. Sometimes it is spontaneous, sometimes as a result of prayer, and sometimes it follows a laying on of hands. We cannot discount God's prerogative to heal diseases and physical maladies today. What is in question is the "gift" of healing. If someone had the gift of healing today on the scale that existed in the New Testament, there would be no question about it. "The most we can say of charismatic healers is that at some moments and in some respects they are enabled to perform like the gifted healers of New Testament times, and every such occasion confirms that God's touch still has its ancient power. But that is much less than saying that in the ministry of these folk the New Testament gift of healing reappears" (Packer 214).

Prophecy: New Testament prophecy was twofold. First, prophets spoke forth the word of God in power. Second, some prophets some of the time were able to tell the future, or give direct revelation from God. Looking only at the first characteristic, we have prophets today in the New Testament sense. But if you include telling the future or giving direct revelation, then the gift of prophecy does not exist as a restoration of the New Testament gift. Being able to speak confidently like Jeremiah, with the statement, "Thus sayeth the Lord," is not convincingly established in the charismatic movement.

Exorcisms: Packer does not address the issue of exorcisms.

In summary, according to Packer's view, it cannot be convincingly concluded that the New Testament gifts have, after a period of dormancy, been given back to the church *just as they were*. Nor can it be convincingly concluded that the gifts have endured since New Testament times and are revived to New Testament levels. Neither of these views is supported from Scripture or experience. If we want to discern what God may be doing in the Pentecostal, charismatic, and third wave movements, we must think about it in other terms. We must explain what is going on in some way *other* than to say that the New Testament miraculous gifts are fully restored.

If they are not the restored gifts, what are they? Packer asserts that the newer charismatic movement at the leadership level is less dogmatic about issues such as a distinctive view of baptism of the Holy Spirit, speaking in tongues, and so forth, viewing them not so much as hard requirements for salvation or a mature Christian life, but increasingly as sanctified natural abilities (Packer 221). As such, he views what God is doing among charismatics today as being "essentially what **God is working to renew Christ's image in each believer.** he is doing in the lives of all believing, regenerate people everywhere—namely, working to renew Christ's image in each, so that trust, love, hope, patience, commitment, loyalty, self-denial and self-giving, obedience and joy, may increasingly be seen in us" (Packer 222).

Variations

There are variations on the "Approximation" position, and it is important to understand that those who do not experience or practice miraculous gifts do not have a unified position on them or have just one way to explain some of the more unusual things that sometimes happen. It is a struggle for many believers to reconcile, as much as is possible, the apparently contradictory claims made by otherwise godly and credible people on both sides of the "signs and wonders" issue.

Two variations on the "Approximation" position are the "Sovereignty" view and the "Duplication" view. These two views are essentially within the Approximation camp, but have different elements and emphases.

The Sovereignty view distinguishes between miraculous gifts and God's sovereign choice to act and perform miracles. This position emphasizes that God is certainly working miracles today. He is healing and doing other extraordinary things, but He is doing them through His sovereign choice, not through people possessing miraculous spiritual gifts. Sometimes He acts in response to prayer and extraordinary faith, but other times He simply chooses when and what miracle He will perform.

Godly and credible people hold divergent views.

According to this view, the presence of a spiritual gift would manifest itself in a highly consistent success rate, like those with the gift of healing in the New Testament. It is true that there are instances in the New Testament when a gifted person was unsuccessful. For example, even Jesus, when He returned to His hometown of Nazareth, "did not do many miracles there because of their unbelief" (Matthew 13:58). And it is also true that a person who is not gifted might see miracles in his ministry. Nevertheless, the issue is consistency. The possession of a gift would offer a much higher degree of consistency and obvious success than we see today. Certainly, some extraordinary things are going on in the church around the world, but they are being done, according to this view, not through individuals who have miraculous gifts, but through the sovereign action of God. When this sovereign action of God occurs frequently in the ministry of some individuals, it may give the appearance that the individual through whom God is working has a miraculous gift.

The second view, the Duplication view, holds that miraculous gifts and signs and wonders had a primary lasting purpose of validating the new message of salvation by grace through faith in Christ (Hebrews 2:3–4) and that whenever the circumstances that called for the original miraculous gifts and signs and wonders are duplicated, the miraculous gifts and signs and wonders could reappear. In the same vein, if the circumstances that called for the original signs and wonders are approximated but not duplicated, you would see an approximation of the signs and wonders but not a duplication, which makes it, in that case, virtually identical to the Approximation view. The Duplication view differs from the Approximation view by holding out the possibility of a full reinstatement of miraculous gifts and signs and wonders if there is a full duplication of the circumstances that called for them originally. The difference is largely a matter of degree.

It might be helpful to clarify what is meant by "a duplication of the circumstances that called for the original gifts." The original circumstances were that a new message of salvation was being proclaimed to people who had never heard it before. Christianity was not established, the Bible was not recognized, there was much resistance to the new message by established religious leaders who were against any new religion, and there was demonic resistance. If these circumstances reappeared, there might be a reappearance of the miraculous gifts, according to this view.

The early church faced a hostile, unbelieving environment.

Let us suppose, for example, that a missionary makes contact with people in the heart of the rain forest in the Philippines. These people have never seen a Caucasian before; they know nothing of electricity or aviation or world politics or anything of the modern world. They are completely cut off from modern life. They have never heard the name of God, they have never heard of Jesus, and not only have they never heard of the Bible, they can't even read. Their language has never been reduced to writing. They are entirely ignorant of anything that might predispose them to believe in Christianity.

They are, however, very religious. They worship a spirit that they believe inhabits a huge tree. Every day, one of the villagers must sacrifice a chicken on a rock at the base of the tree, and once a year, on the new year, they must sacrifice a pig. If they don't, they are convinced that terrible things will happen to them. Their sacrifice is a distinct hardship on them, because it is expensive. That's 364 chickens and one pig a year taken out of their village economy. They need those animals to feed themselves, yet they sacrifice them to the "cause" so that something worse will not happen to them.

In this context, along comes a missionary who says, "You don't have to sacrifice these animals to the tree god any more. Jesus is more powerful than the tree god, and He will keep you safe." The villagers eye the missionary suspiciously. They would like to believe him, but do they dare? What if the missionary is wrong? What if this new God, whom they have never heard of, know nothing about, and have seen no evidence of, is not stronger than the tree god? What if the missionary, who has very little credibility with them because he is an outsider, is wrong? There is no way of knowing if his word can be trusted. The missionary has never felt the wrath of the tree god.

This situation would be, in principle, a duplication of the environment that called for the sign gifts in the Bible. If miraculous gifts and signs and wonders accompanied the new message, it would give the villagers a foundation for belief. They would be believing "something" rather than "nothing," just as in the New Testament story.

If the circumstances were less extreme, but approximated the New Testament conditions, then the miraculous ministry might be approximated, which, as was stated earlier, makes this view virtually identical to the Approximation view.

Evaluation

This position has its problems, too. Much of the Approximation view is built on arguments from silence. It takes the silence of Scripture and begins making conceivable arguments of probability that are then read back into Scripture. For example, the statement, "There is nothing in the Bible that explicitly states that the miraculous gifts and signs and wonders cannot re-emerge if the circumstances that called for them originally are duplicated," is true; but it also rests on what the Bible does *not* say, not on what it does say.

Conclusion

We see, then, that no matter what position you take on this matter, there are problems with it. Unfortunately, we do not have the option of an airtight view held by all evangelical believers. Whatever position we take, therefore, it must accommodate what the Bible teaches, and it must integrate the experiences of mature believers, and it must accommodate the Scriptural injunction to "preserve the unity of the Spirit in the bond of peace" (Ephesians 4:3 NASB).

Though each side of the signs and wonders issue has its strengths and weaknesses, each side seems fully prepared to champion its strengths and defend its weaknesses to the other side. But it is like one of the books I reviewed in preparation to write this chapter, entitled *Five Views on Sanctification*, by five different authors. Sanctification means, essentially, spiritual growth after becoming a Christian. The format for the book was very creative. Author #1 presented his understanding of sanctification, and then authors #2–#5 gave a rebuttal of his view. Then, author #2 gave his position on sanctification, and authors #1 and #3–#5 gave their rebuttals, and so on. I was less than halfway through before my pupils dilated wildly and my eyeballs began rotating slowly in their sockets. The variables on that many positions and that many rebuttals are astonishing. All four authors #2–#5 were against what author #1 wrote, but for *four* different reasons! Such a presentation verifies for me that no problem is so difficult but that, if you look at it hard enough, long enough, and with bright enough minds, it can become even more difficult!

Such is the case with the "signs and wonders" vs. "no signs and wonders" positions. The "signs and wonders" people sometimes look at the others and say that they are straight as a gun barrel theologically and just as empty spiritually. The "no signs and wonders" people sometimes look at the others and say that they have put their minds in their hip pockets and are reading subjective experiences back into the biblical text.

By a fuller understanding of the issues, we might be able to experience greater legitimate unity in the future. If we can hold each other's spiritual and intellectual integrity in greater re-

Spiritual name-calling does not advance the gospel.

spect, we might find that our position (whatever it happens to be) might not be the only possible interpretation, and we can find greater unity than if we take our conclusions, press them to the extreme, and attack one another as enemies. This is not to say that it is wrong to disagree with others on biblical interpretation. That is inevitable. But if we earnestly try, we might find more things on which we agree, fewer things about which we must be dogmatic, and present our convictions in a way that upholds the integrity of others, rather than attacking those with whom we do not agree.

The person and doctrine of the Holy Spirit is so central to spiritual life and growth that it is often not possible for one church to satisfy everyone. But that is all right. No one church is going to be right for everyone. We also must admit that on both sides of the issue there are immature, over-opinionated, and sanctimonius individuals with whom it is difficult to foster fellowship.

However, with such great enemies outside the church, we can hardly afford the luxury of infighting over things for which there is room for responsible and enlightened disagreement. If it is a matter that affects salvation or the integrity of Scripture, or another doctrine on which we cannot get "soft" without endangering the integrity of the Christian message, then we dare not compromise. No one should ever compromise on an issue of fundamental importance. But if well-meaning, spiritually mature, well-educated Christians who agree on the essentials of the Christian faith happen to disagree on matters within that overall unity, then we can search for greater understanding and unity. Whether it is the issues between Calvinists and Arminians, dispensationalists and the Reformed, or charismatic or noncharismatic, these points of contention often divide people who are clearly Christian. On these matters, we would do well to "endeavor to keep the unity of the Spirit in the bond of peace" (Ephesians 4:3).

Outside the gate are camped Islamic fundamentalism, Eastern religions, the New Age movement, secularism and secular humanism, animism, voodoo, Satanism, witchcraft, the occult, materialism, hedonism (the pursuit of pleasure), and an explosion of cults. These oppose the gospel itself, not merely an interpretation of a few dimensions of the Christian life and ministry. In our disputes within the faith, we are sometimes like soldiers in the trenches, swatting each other for stepping on our spitpolished shoes, while the invading hordes are cresting the nearest hill. It is an old saying, but still true: "In essentials, unity; in nonessentials, diversity; in all things, charity."

Speed Bump!

Slow down long enough to be sure you've gotten the main points of this chapter.

Question
Answer

Q1. What is the Durative position?

A1. The Durative position is the belief that the signs and wonders in the New Testament have continued throughout church history and still exist *today*.

Q2. What is the Cessationist position?

A2. The Cessationist position states that New Testament signs and wonders *disappeared* with the passing of the apostles and the establishment of the Scriptures and are not intended ever to reappear again.

Q3. What is the Approximation position?

A3. The Approximation position holds that the miraculous gifts and signs and wonders are not fully operative today, but that a *reduced* form of the gifts operates today under the apparent blessing of God.

Fill in the Blank

Question
Answer

Q1. What is the Durative position?

A1. The Durative position is the belief that the signs and wonders in the New Testament have continued throughout church history and still exist _____.

Q2. What is the Cessationist position?

A2. The Cessationist position states that New Testament signs and wonders _____ with the passing of the apostles and the establishment of the Scriptures and are not intended ever to reappear again.

Q3. What is the Approximation position?

A3. The Approximation position holds that the miraculous gifts and signs and wonders are not fully operative today, but that a _____ form of the gifts operates today under the apparent blessing of God.

For Further Discussion and Thought

1. Do you think it is possible for those who believe in signs and wonders and those who do not to coexist in harmony in the same church, since both view their positions as coming from Scripture?

2. If you do, how?

3. If you don't, how do you think Christians can preserve the unity of the Spirit in the bond of peace, even though there is deep disagreement on this issue?

What if I Don't Believe?

Since there are so many positions held by godly and knowledgeable people within Christendom concerning signs and wonders, it is not a surprise that there are several popular positions among church members. It is important that we hold our positions with biblical conviction and Christlike regard for others who may hold an alternative opinion.

For Further Study

1. Scripture
- John 17:20–23
- Romans 12:4–8
- 1 Corinthians 12:4–8
- 1 Corinthians 12:23–27
- Ephesians 4:1–16
- Read these passages and consider how they add to your understanding of this subject.

2. Books
Several other books are very helpful in studying this subject. The following will provide a wide variety of perspectives to help you gain a fuller understanding of this challenging subject.

The Holy Spirit, Billy Graham
Keep in Step with the Spirit, James I. Packer
The Third Wave of the Holy Spirit, C. Peter Wagner
Power Religion, Michael Horton* (written from the traditional evangelical viewpoint)
The Kingdom and the Power, Gary Greig and Kevin Springer* (written from the Pentecostal/charismatic viewpoint)

* These are very thorough books written from opposite positions.

The Holy Spirit expects us to take seriously
the answers he has already provided, the light
he has already shed; and he does not expect us
to plead for things that have already been
denied.
■ **Paul Little**

8

What Does It Mean to Be Filled With the Holy Spirit?

It is said that the Eskimos have something like forty-seven words in their language for the word we know as "snow." For those living in warmer regions, if it's white and cold, it's snow. But for the Eskimo, understanding the various words for "snow" can make a difference between life and death.

For example, they might have a word like "fliff-fluff" for the light, fluffy, powdery kind of snow that floats softly to earth and gently covers everything with a pristine blanket of dazzling white—perfect for photographs and Christmas cards. Or, they might have a word like "screamin-freezer" for the bitter kind of storm-driven, horizontal, freeze-your-eyebrows-off stuff that howls for days and buries everything under an avalanche of white death.

Now, let's say you are a missionary to the Eskimos, newly arrived, so you speak only English. You have been spending the afternoon with an Eskimo family. Through a translator you've been able to communicate with these new friends. When it's time to leave and you don your gear, Father Eskimo says, "It is going to fliff-fluff." You don't understand, so you lean over to your translator and ask, "What did he say?" The translator replies, "He says it's going to snow."

"I'm not afraid of a little snow," you think, so you head for home. As you walk, powdery flakes begin drifting to earth, blanketing the ground in a foot of brilliant white. "Oh, this is lovely!" you say. "It's like walking home through a Currier and Ives painting."

A week later you are visiting in the home of another local family, and as you get ready to leave the Eskimo says, "It is going to screamin-freezer." You've learned a number of words already, but this is a new one. "What did he say?" you ask. And your translator replies, "He says it's going to snow."

Ah, snow! That delightful, fluffy stuff. It will be nice to walk home in that pristine glory again. So you leave. Suddenly, up comes this sixty-mile-an-hour wind and snow so heavy you can't see your eyelashes. Bitter-cold ice pellets sting your face as you lean forward into the blast. When you finally get home, you think, "Why didn't that guy tell me the weather was going to be so terrible?"

He did, of course, but the translator failed to communicate as precisely as he could have. The word "snow" was correct, but not precise enough to make clear the intensity of this snowstorm.

A similar snag in communication often occurs when Christians study the Bible. At times the Bible will use a word or phrase that is perfectly clear, correct, and sufficiently precise for those to whom it was originally written. These are like the Eskimos who move with nat-

---

In this chapter we learn that . . .

1. The Pentecostal/charismatic interpretation is that the filling of the Spirit here neither requires nor rules out supernormal experiences such as speaking in tongues.
2. The "victorious Christian life" interpretation is that the filling of the Spirit empowers a person for improved Christian living and greater ministry.
3. The "word of Christ" interpretation is that the filling of the Spirit is essentially the same as "letting the word of Christ dwell in you richly.

---

ural ease among their forty-seven words for "snow." But we who read these words or phrases 2,000 years later are like the missionary to the Eskimos that I asked you to imagine yourself being. Because we lack firsthand experience in Bible life and times, we sometimes have to work very hard and use the best scholarly resources to determine the precise meaning of words in parts of the Bible. And even then, well-meaning, devout, and scholarly believers do not agree about what such words do or do not, or may or may not mean in specific Bible passages.

A good example is Ephesians 5:18, where we are commanded to be filled with the Spirit. While a number of verses in the New Testament *mention* the filling of the Holy Spirit, only this one *commands* us to be filled with the Spirit. For that reason, it receives a lot of attention—and there are significantly different understandings of what being filled with the Spirit means. We look at three interpretations of Ephesians 5:18 in this chapter and attempt to summarize a mainstream position within the traditions from which these interpretations come. But beyond noting the differences between these views, we also point to the significant amount of understanding they share. The differences are real and will not go away; nevertheless, we are brothers and sisters in Christ, and there is value in not overlooking our common ground.

What Is the Pentecostal/Charismatic Interpretation of Ephesians 5:18?

The Pentecostal/charismatic interpretation is that the filling of the Spirit here neither requires nor rules out supernormal experiences such as speaking in tongues.

Charismatics (and with them Pentecostal and third wave Christians) believe that Spirit-fillings of the type common in Acts occur today as well, complete with supernormal experiences such as speaking in tongues. Regarding Ephesians 5:18, however, they agree that speaking in tongues and other high-profile manifestations of the Spirit are not mentioned and are not a necessary result of the ongoing infilling of the Spirit, but neither are they ruled out. The term "fullness" is a favorite both in Ephesians (1:10, 23; 3:19; 4:13) and to charismatic believers, and they would urge all believers to yield to the ongoing filling of the Spirit in their lifelong seeking to "be filled with all the fullness of God" (Ephesians 3:19).

Charismatics stress that Ephesians 5:18 should be read keeping in mind all that Acts records about the ministry of the gospel in Ephesus, perhaps only a few years earlier (Acts 19—20). They believe that the context provided by Acts alerts us to ways that Ephesians 5:18–21 may point to "charismatic" activity as a part of the filling of the Spirit here. For example, the close connection between being "filled with the Spirit" (v. 18) and "spiritual songs" invites reference to the charismatic singing described in 1 Corinthians 14:15–16, 26.

In any event, charismatics point out that one consistent result of any Spirit filling is some form of Spirit-inspired speech—whether tongues or prophecy (Acts 2:4; 4:31; 19:6), or "speaking to one another in psalms and hymns and spiritual songs" (Ephesians 5:19). Another result is well-being within the body of Christ—whether the creation of a wholly new community of faith as on the day of Pentecost (Acts 2:46–48), or Christlike service, "submitting to one another in the fear of God" as Ephesians 5:21 directs.

Why do I need to know what it means to be filled with the Holy Spirit?

1. I need to know so that I can experience all that Jesus wants me to experience in my walk with Him.
2. I need to know so that I will not expect something from God that He does not intend to give me.
3. I need to know so that I will not take on a burden that God does not intend for me to carry.
4. I need to know so that I can explain the truth to others.

The charismatic view, then, would be that the filling of the Spirit in view in Ephesians 5:18 results in Spirit-inspired speech (often worship) and service within the body of Christ. It neither requires nor rules out specifically "charismatic" manifestations such as tongues.

What Is the "Victorious Christian Life" Interpretation of Ephesians 5:18?

The "victorious Christian life" interpretation is that the filling of the Spirit empowers a person for improved Christian living and greater ministry.

A second major interpretation is that of the "victorious Christian life." This position maintains that the filling of the Spirit is God's empowering for victorious Christian living and service. It does not result in any miraculous manifestations such as speaking in tongues and prophesying. But it does result in greater power for deliverance from sin, for living a Christian lifestyle and for ministry.

Certain conditions must be met, according to this tradition, in order to be filled; and when these conditions are met, believers are then filled with the Spirit. This filling must be taken by faith, since there are often no immediate observable results. These conditions vary slightly according to different Bible teachers, but usually include the following:

1. Dedicating one's life to the Lord in an initial, crisis-like act in which one gives his life to God for His will to be done through it (Charles Ryrie, *A Survey of Bible Doctrine* 83). This initial dedication must be followed by a lifestyle of continual dedication to the will of God and daily dependence on the Holy Spirit.
2. Confessing sin and putting away any sins that you are harboring in your life;
3. Asking to be filled; and
4. Believing that God did, indeed, fill with His Spirit, even though one may see or feel no evidence of it.

What Is the "Word of Christ" Interpretation of Ephesians 5:18?

The "word of Christ" interpretation is that the filling of the Spirit is essentially the same as "letting the word of Christ dwell in you richly."

According to this view, the results of being filled with the Spirit in Ephesians 5:18 are the same as the results of "letting the word of Christ dwell in you richly" in Colossians 3:16. Therefore, since the consequences are the same, they are seen as essentially the same thing.

In Ephesians 5:19—6:6 the results of being filled with the Spirit are

- speaking in psalms,
- singing,
- giving thanks,
- and a harmony of relationships between husbands and wives, parents and children, masters and slaves.

In Colossians 3:16–22 we see the same results:

- teaching with psalms,
- singing,
- thankfulness,
- and harmony between husbands and wives, parents and children, masters and slaves.

The results in Colossians are produced, however, not by being filled with the Spirit, but by "let[ting] the word of Christ dwell in you richly." Being *filled with the Spirit* and *letting the word of Christ dwell in you* produce exactly the same results. Therefore, careful attention must be paid to the possible link between the two.

The "word of Christ" in Colossians 3:16 does not refer explicitly to the New Testament, because the New Testament had not all been written yet. It refers, however, to that which was known to the Colossians about Jesus and His teachings, even though the New Testament was not yet complete. By implication, today it would apply to the entire Bible, with a special emphasis on the central place Christ's ministry and teachings hold.

To allow the word of Christ to dwell within us, we must read the word of God, study it, memorize it, and meditate on it, with a spirit of obedience. As we do, the Holy Spirit illumines the truth of the Scripture to us (1 Corinthians 2:9–16); convicts us of sin (John 16:8); strengthens us for righteous living and worship (Ephesians 3:14–21); and nurtures His fruit within us so that we experience love, joy, peace, longsuffering, kindness, goodness, faithfulness, gentleness, and self-control (Galatians 5:22–23). As this process begins, grows, and bears fruit, we are filled with the Spirit.

What Happens When We are Filled With the Spirit?

There are four primary results when we are filled with the Holy Spirit: I involve myself in mutual ministry to others, We experience inner joy, I cultivate an attitude of gratitude, and I live in a spirit of mutual submission to others.

While all three of the above traditions might not agree on all the possible conditions for being filled with the Spirit or all the possible results, they do agree on the ones listed in the Ephesians 5 passage. The consequence of the Spirit-filled life is a heart that desires to minister to others . . . a heart that experiences joy . . . a heart that is grateful . . . and a heart that serves.

Mutual Ministry

speaking to one another in psalms and hymns and spiritual songs.   Ephesians 5:19

Christians are not to be rugged individualists, standing alone, or as islands unto themselves. Nor are we to erect barriers between ourselves and others, daring them to cross. As part of the body of Christ, we need others, and others need us.

Each of us has been gifted to minister to others, and we are responsible to exercise that gift. Some of us, of course, have been called by God to labor vocationally in ministry. But God intends for all of us to minister when opportunity arises—in our workplaces, in our neighborhoods, in our families, and in our society. Realizing that we have this personal responsibility and then having a heart to help others is a mark of being filled with the Holy Spirit.

God intends for each believer to minister to others.

The totality of all believers—all true Christians—is called the body of Christ. The human body is a picture of that spiritual body. By observing how the human body functions, we gain insight into how the spiritual body should function.

For example, consider the cooperation of the entire body involved when a toddler takes his first steps:

> If we traced all the body signals involved in walking, we would find in that grinning, perilously balanced toddler a machine of unfathomable complexity. Over one hundred million sense cells in each eye compose a picture of the table he is walking toward. Stretch receptors in the neck relate the attitude of his head to the trunk and maintain appropriate muscle tension. Joint receptors fire off messages that report the angles of limb bones. The sense organs inside the ear inform the brain of the direction of gravity and the body's balance. Pressure from the ground on each toe triggers messages about the type of surface on which he is walking. . . . A casual glance down to avoid a toy on the carpet will cause all these sense organs to shift dramatically; the image of the ground moves rapidly across the retina, but the inner ear and stretch receptors assure the brain the body is not falling. Any movement of the head alters the body's center of gravity, affecting the tension in each of the limb muscles. The toddler's body crackles with millions of messages informing his brain and giving directions to perform the extraordinary feat of walking (Paul Brand and Philip Yancey, *Fearfully and Wonderfully Made*).

When seen up close, in detail, the physical act of walking is a stupefying miracle. When seen up close, in detail, the spiritual act of "walking together" is an equally stupefying miracle. It requires millions of individual beings, contaminated by the impulse to act independently, to reject that impulse and subordinate themselves to the leading of Jesus, the Head, and move in concert with His will rather than millions of individual wills. The miracle of spiritual unity is no less awesome than the miracle of physical unity.

Lone rangers are not filled with the Spirit. Human islands are not filled with the Spirit. Human porcupines are not filled with the Holy Spirit.

Those who are filled with the Holy Spirit sense the importance of mutual ministry. They understand that they are part of a larger whole, and they see the need for unity with the Head and the body of which they are a part.

Out of that sense of wholeness the Spirit-filled life finds joy.

Inner Joy
Singing and making melody in your heart to the Lord.
Ephesians 5:19

You need not have a beautiful voice to have a beautiful heart. Yet when the Holy Spirit invades your heart, inner joy expresses itself in inner song. And this inner joy does not depend on circumstances. It survives in spite of circumstances.

In his book *Winning over Pain, Fear and Worry,* John Haggai tells how his son suffered severe physical trauma at birth because the doctor, a respected obstetrician, was intoxicated at the time.

> During the first year of the little lad's life, eight doctors said he could not possibly survive. For the first two years of his life, my wife had to feed him every three hours with a Brecht feeder. It took a half hour to prepare for the feeding and it took another half hour to clean up and put him back to bed. Not once during that time did she ever get out of the house for any diversion whatsoever. Never did she get more than two hours sleep at one time.
>
> My wife, Christine, had once been acclaimed by some of the nation's leading musicians as one of the outstanding contemporary female vocalists in America. From the time she was thirteen she had been popular as a singer—and constantly in the public eye. Hers was the experience of receiving and rejecting some fancy offers with even fancier incomes to marry an aspiring Baptist pastor with no church to pastor!
>
> Then, after five years of marriage, the tragedy struck! . . . She was now marooned within the walls of our home. Her beautiful voice no longer enraptured public audiences. (414)

Although John Edmund, Jr., was paralyzed, able to sit in his wheelchair only with the assistance of full-length body braces, his parents rejoiced to have him with them for over twenty years—and rejoiced that he committed his heart and life to Jesus Christ and evidenced genuine concern for the things of the Lord.

I attribute his commitment to Jesus Christ and his wonderful disposition to the sparkling radiance of an emotionally mature, Christ-centered mother who has mastered the discipline of living one day at a time. Never have I—nor has anyone else—heard a word of complaint from her. (415)

Ah, God's mercy. Sometimes it is so severe. Yet the Spirit-filled life is a life of joy, surviving not because of the circumstances, but in spite of them.

I believe that some people, like Christine Haggai, are gifted to respond to music more than others. But everyone who is filled with the Spirit will enjoy and appreciate the music of the soul that lifts his or her heart to God.

And out of that joy the Spirit-filled heart gives thanks.

Gratitude
Giving thanks always for all things to God the Father in the name of our Lord Jesus Christ.   Ephesians 5:20

When we trace the word "thanksgiving" through the Bible—both the Old and New Testaments—we get a sense of God's attitude toward gratitude. Consider just a few passages:

For in the days of David and Asaph, in ancient times, there were leaders of the singers, songs of praise and hymns of thanksgiving to God.   Nehemiah 12:46 (NASB)

I will praise the name of God with song, and shall magnify Him with thanksgiving.   Psalm 69:30 (NASB)

Let us come before His presence with thanksgiving; Let us shout joyfully to Him with psalms.   Psalm 95:2

Enter into His gates with thanksgiving, And into His courts with praise. Be thankful to Him, and bless His name.   Psalm 100:4

Blessing and glory and wisdom, thanksgiving and honor and power and might, be to our God forever and ever. Amen.

Revelation 7:12

With this kind of emphasis, it is little wonder that the third manifestation of the filling of the Holy Spirit is a grateful heart. Having 20/20 spiritual sight, the Spirit-filled heart is thankful.

If we understood how perilously our lives hang in the balance as we go about our daily routine, if we understood how vigorous the spiritual warfare is around us, if we understood how fortunate we are to have food on the table, a roof over our heads, and clothes on our backs, if we grasped how dependent we are on the common grace of God and the goodness of others for our basic necessities in life, we would be grateful people. We would be grateful for what we do have, rather than ungrateful for what we do not have. If we truly grasped our sin, and that it is because of the Lord's mercies that we are not consumed (Lamentations 3:22), yes, we would be more grateful.

Finally, the heart that ministers to others, beating with joy and thanksgiving, is truly the heart of a servant.

A Servant Heart

Submitting to one another in the fear of God.   Ephesians 5:21

Anyone who knows anything about chickens knows that there is a pecking order in the barnyard. There is a Top Chicken, who can peck any other chicken in the barnyard without fear of reprisal. And there is a Bottom Chicken, who can't peck anybody without fear of reprisal. All the other chickens are aligned in a hierarchy of power between these two.

If a kernel of corn falls between any two chickens, the one with a higher pecking order gets the kernel. If there is any question as to which is which, a fracas breaks out—anywhere from a skirmish to all-out war. When the fight is over, the winner establishes or reestablishes dominance over the other, and the hierarchy adjusts itself accordingly from top to bottom.

The same order can be observed in the great chicken coop of life. In the various coops we frequent (job, school, church, neighborhood, etc.) there are top humans and bottom humans, and all in between are aligned in a hierarchy of power—a great human pecking order.

If an opportunity for advancement falls between two humans, a fracas breaks out—anywhere from a little skirmish to all-out war. This can mean anything from dirty looks to murder, whereby humans establish dominance over other humans, and the hierarchy is established.

Just as chickens constantly jockey for position in the barnyard pecking order, so humans constantly jockey for power in the chicken coop of life. It is only natural. As Christians, however, we are not to participate in this great posturing for position. We are not to act naturally; we are to act supernaturally.

Power struggles are not consistent with Christ's kingdom.

A case in point occurred when James and John, two brothers who were Christ's disciples, began jockeying for position in the coming kingdom (Mark 10:35–45). "Master," they said, "when your kingdom comes, let one of us sit on your right hand and the other on your left." They wanted to be top chickens in the kingdom of God.

"Men, you have it all wrong," Jesus replied. "That's the way the world acts. They love to lord it over others. But things are entirely different in My kingdom. In My kingdom, if you want to be great, you must become a servant to everyone else."

What a shock! In heaven, the pecking order is reversed. The first shall be last and the last shall be first. Those who humble themselves, God exalts. Those who exalt themselves, God humbles.

"For even the Son of Man did not come to be served, but to serve, and to give His life a ransom for many (Mark 10:45).

Conclusion

Corrie ten Boom, a Dutch Christian who was imprisoned in a German concentration camp during World War II for helping and hiding Jews in the Netherlands, wrote in her marvelous book, *Tramp for the Lord*:

The war was over. Even before I left the concentration camp, I knew I would be busy helping those who had lost their way. Now

I found myself starting just such a work in Bloemendaal (Holland). It was more than a home for the homeless; it was a refuge for those who had lost their way spiritually as well as physically.

Yet, because I had lived so close to death, looking it in the face day after day, I often felt like a stranger among my own people—many of whom looked upon money, honor of men, and success as the important issues of life. Standing in front of a crematorium, knowing that any day could be your last day, gives one a different perspective on life. The words of an old German motto kept flashing in my mind:

"What I spend, I had; what I saved, I lost; what I gave, I have."

How well I understood the feeling of the artist who painted the picture of the corpse of a once wealthy man and entitled it, *Sic transit gloria mundi*—So passes the glory of this world. The material things of this world no longer excited me—nor would they ever again. (29)

When we are filled with the Spirit, we get our eyes off this world and onto the Lord.

Though there are differences among Christians in their understandings of what it means to be filled with the Spirit, there are also common beliefs, and there is great value in highlighting these common beliefs. Mature Christians of all three of the above traditions would agree that our task is to yield to the Spirit of God, to worship God in spirit and in truth, and to build up the community He creates by serving one another in the way Christ served all (Philippians 2:1–16).

Our task is to yield to the Spirit of God.

Christians of all three traditions would agree that we should cultivate an awareness of the presence of the Spirit within us to be alert to His leading, His convicting, His illuminating ministry, and to be ready to follow Him in total obedience. We must be responsive to Him when He moves in our lives in extraordinary ways and leads us to worship the Lord and serve Him with unusual anointing. We must live in relationship to the Holy Spirit and allow Him to have His way in our lives. Whatever the filling of the Holy Spirit means, it must surely include the things that Christians agree on.

Speed Bump!

Slow down to be sure you've gotten the main points of this chapter.

Question
Answer

Q1. What is the Pentecostal/charismatic interpretation of Ephesians 5:18?

A1. The Pentecostal/charismatic interpretation is that the filling of the Spirit here neither requires nor rules out super-normal *experiences* such as speaking in tongues.

Q2. What is the "victorious Christian life" interpretation of Ephesians 5:18?

A2. The "victorious Christian life" interpretation is that the filling of the Spirit *empowers* a person for improved Christian living and greater ministry.

Q3. What is the "word of Christ" interpretation of Ephesians 5:18?

A3. The "word of Christ" interpretation is that the filling of the Spirit is essentially the same as "letting the *word* of Christ dwell in you richly."

Fill in the Blank

Question
Answer

Q1. What is the Pentecostal/charismatic interpretation of Ephesians 5:18?

A1. The Pentecostal/charismatic interpretation is that the filling of the Spirit here neither requires nor rules out super-normal _____ such as speaking in tongues.

Q2. What is the "victorious Christian life" interpretation of Ephesians 5:18?

A2. The "victorious Christian life" interpretation is that the filling of the Spirit _____ a person for improved Christian living and greater ministry.

Q3. What is the "word of Christ" interpretation of Ephesians 5:18?

A3. The "word of Christ" interpretation is that the filling of the Spirit is essentially the same as "letting the _____ of Christ dwell in you richly."

For Further Thought and Discussion

1. There are four characteristics of being filled with the Spirit. Two have to do with music: (1) speaking to one another in psalms, hymns, and spiritual songs, and (2) singing and making melody in your heart to the Lord. How could we more completely encourage these activities today?

2. Gratitude to the Lord and a spirit of deference to one another are two other characteristics of being filled with the Holy Spirit. How easily do these characteristics come to you naturally? What do you think you could do to encourage them in your life?

3. When you look at the things on which all Christians agree regarding the filling of the Spirit, do you see those things in your life to the degree you would like? If not, what do you think you could do to experience a fuller walk with the Lord?

What If I Don't Believe?

If I don't believe that the filling of the Holy Spirit results, over time, in mutual ministry, inner joy, gratitude, and a servant heart, then several negative things result. First, I have no standard by which to measure my spiritual progress. Second, I may not consider these four things important and therefore may be content with a personal character that is devoid of these things. Third, I may never experience the joy that comes from the filling of the Spirit. Finally, my life will be a disappointment to God, who commands me to be filled with the Spirit and who longs for me to experience the fellowship and joy of the Spirit.

For Further Study

1. Scripture

- Mark 10:42–45
- John 15:7–11
- Acts 2:1–21
- Romans 8:1–17
- Galatians 5:16–23

- Galatians 6:10
- Ephesians 5:17–21
- Colossians 3:16–22
- 1 Thessalonians 5:18

2. Books
A number of books are helpful on this subject. In reading them, however, you will discover great diversity among the authors.

Flying Closer to the Flame, Charles Swindoll
I Believe in the Holy Spirit, Michael Green
Keep in Step with the Spirit, James I. Packer
Joy Unspeakable, Martin Lloyd-Jones
30 Days to Understanding How to Live as a Christian, Max Anders
Spirit-filled, Jack Hayford

Sin is like ice in our pipes—our spiritual lives have been "frozen." There is only one solution, and that is repentance to clear the blockage and restore the flow of the Holy Spirit.
■ Billy Graham

What Is the Unpardonable Sin?

I mentioned in an earlier chapter that I struggled a bit with assurance of my salvation when I first became a Christian. I had told a friend who was a Christian about my conversion, thinking my friend would be happy for me. But my friend wasn't convinced that I was truly a Christian. That shook me, and took me many years to completely get over. Complicating the impact of that experience was my inconsistency as a Christian. I had a lot of hang-ups when I came to Christ. On the outside, I looked like a clean-cut, all-American boy. Inside, I was a bedlam of insecurities, inadequacies, inferiorities, competitions, comparisons, resentments, and instabilities.

I was in college when I became a Christian, and I remember practicing saying "hi" to other students when I met them on campus. I would look in the mirror and say "hi" over and over again, trying to get it right. I tried to get my facial expression just right, exuding confidence. I would deepen my voice as much as I could, trying to sound like a rich baritone, which I wasn't. I also was painfully aware that my ears stuck out too far, I had a bump in the bridge of my nose, and I was too skinny.

When playing basketball, I often exploded in anger if things didn't go right. If someone started playing well, rather than being happy for him, I resented him for threatening my position.

I didn't want to be this way. I prayed and read my Bible faithfully. I went to church, attended prayer meetings, revival meetings, and special Bible studies. I shared my faith, taught Sunday school, and did everything I knew to do; but still I didn't grow spiritually as fast as I thought I should, and I didn't understand why. What else could I do?

I was already doing more than most of the other people on that Christian college campus.

I used to say, "Lord, spiritually, I want to be more than I am, and in reading the Bible it is clear that you want me to be more than I am. So why am I not making more progress?"

Finally, I decided I wasn't committed enough. I would really throw myself into it. I would read my Bible an hour a day, and I would pray an hour a day. That ought to do it. So I did that for the remainder of that semester. At the end of the semester, I was more out of fellow-

---

In this chapter we learn that . . .

1. We cannot sin so often that God will not forgive us.
2. We cannot sin so badly that God will not forgive us.
3. The unpardonable sin is rejecting the Holy Spirit's pull to bring us to Christ.

---

ship than when I began. I'm not exactly sure what I expected. Perhaps I expected my face to glow when I emerged from my prayer time. Perhaps I thought that I might walk slightly above the ground. At least I thought I could quit being so crabby and resentful.

I would go to my prayer time and say, "Lord, I sinned today (at that time in my life, the sin was usually anger). I am sorry. Please forgive me." Then I would go out and sin in anger again. The next day I would say, "Lord, I sinned again today. It was the same sin as yesterday. I am sorry. Please forgive me. I won't do it again." Then I would go out and sin in anger again. The next day, I would say, "Lord, I sinned again today, and I am really, really sorry. I promise you, I won't do it again." Then I would go out and sin again in anger. Then I would come to the Lord and say, "Lord, I sinned again. I know I told you I wouldn't do it again, and I did. But this time, I really mean it. I promise you, I won't do it again." And I would go out and do it again.

I read in James 1:19–20 (NASB), "Let everyone be quick to hear, slow to speak and slow to anger; for the anger of man does not achieve the righteousness of God." I assumed that, because of my continual failure in that area, the name "Max Anders" must bring a noxious odor to the nostrils of God. I envisioned Him standing in heaven, arms crossed, tapping His foot, and heaving a weary sigh, wondering when I was going to get it together.

Finally, I gave up. I thought, "What's the use? It is impossible. I have hit my head against a brick wall so many times I can't hit it again.

The Christian life may work for everyone else, but it does not work for me. I must be inherently spiritually defective." And with that, I quit. I quit praying. I quit reading my Bible. I quit pursuing God. I said, "God, I've given it my best shot, and my best shot wasn't good enough for You. So if You ever come to the point that You want to do something with my life, let me know. I am willing and ready. But until that time, call me; I won't be calling you."

Why I need to know this

I need to know that if I accept Christ's offer of salvation, I cannot commit the unpardonable sin, no matter how badly or how often I sin. God does not want me to sin, but His grace is equal to my sin as long as I am in Christ. If I have not yet accepted Christ's offer of salvation, I still can do so, no matter what my sins are. I can come to Him at any time, and He will not turn me out.

Those were pretty bold words for a creature to say to his Creator. But I was at the end of my rope. Somewhere during this time, someone mentioned something to me about the unpardonable sin. I said, "You mean there is an unpardonable sin?" My friend said, "Oh, yes . . ." He started to go on, but I shouted him down. "Don't tell me! I don't want to know!" I was sure that if I learned what the unpardonable sin was, I would do it. If I didn't know what it was, I might not think of it.

My friend proceeded to explain it to me, and assured me that I could not commit it. I had already avoided it. I heaved the mother of all sighs of relief. Time passed, and by God's grace I began to mature and leave behind the worst of my immaturities, but I have always been grateful not to have committed a sin God could not forgive.

The Bible teaches that there is an unpardonable sin. We want to look at it, to understand what it is, as well as what it isn't. We also want to look at the general subject of sin, to make sure we understand our relationship, as people who commit sin, with the Holy Spirit, who is sinless.

Can We Sin so Often that God Will Not Forgive Us?

We cannot sin so often that God will not forgive us.

The apostle Peter did us a great favor. He flew off the handle. He exaggerated. He lied. He cursed. He chickened out of things.

He broke his word. He manipulated. And not just to men, but also to God. He told Jesus he would do things that he didn't do. He told Him that he would stick with Him to the end. He didn't. He ended up hiding in the shadows while Jesus was taken to the cross.

I do not rejoice in Peter's sin. I wish for him that he had not committed those sins. But he did, and in doing so, he taught us something terribly important. All of us have some of Peter's blood flowing in our veins. All of us have lied, broken our word, gotten angry, and denied Jesus, either directly or indirectly. We feel terrible about it—so bad that sometimes we question whether or not we are even true Christians. Or we get so hopelessly frustrated that we give up trying.

Once I became convinced that I really had become a Christian, I did not struggle much with doubt, but I still became so frustrated with my sin that I gave up. Why? Because all anyone ever told me (with good motives, I'm sure) was that I shouldn't sin, and that God would give me the power to overcome my sin. Yet I didn't see it happening, at least not at the pace that I thought it should.

The issue of how God gives us the power to overcome our sin, and how we should interpret it if we don't seem to be making it is addressed in another book in this series. But what I want to focus on here is whether or not we can out-sin God's patience. Peter proved to us that we cannot.

We all are a bit like Peter.

In the eighteenth chapter of the Gospel of Matthew, beginning with verse 21, Peter asked Jesus, "How often shall my brother sin against me, and I forgive him? Up to seven times?" My guess is that someone had sinned against Peter several times and he had had it. Perhaps he was looking for an out, a way to deal with this person who had sinned against him more than once. He must have reached for the highest number imaginable to him at the moment. He may even have thought that this number was going to impress Jesus or the other disciples who heard him ask the question. I can even hear him clearing his throat before he gives the Big Number. "How often shall my brother sin against me and I forgive him? Up to (ahem) seven times?"

Think about that. Not to give Peter too hard a time, seven is a lot of times if the seven times occur very close together. Peter was being more gracious and forbearing than a lot of us. How many times do you forgive drivers who cut in front of you in traffic? How many times do you forgive a waiter or waitress who is rude to you? How many times do you forgive a friend or family member who says something unkind to you? In those terms, seven seems like a lot.

In spite of that, Jesus said, "I do not say to you up to seven times, but up to seventy times seven." I don't think Jesus meant 490 times. Rather, I think He meant "as often as it happens." If that is the standard to which God holds us, would He not also hold to that standard? That is, if God expects us to forgive a person as many times as that person asks us to forgive him, would not God forgive us as many times as we ask Him?

You see, back in college when I was struggling so hard to be a good Christian and failing so miserably, *I was really trying!* A two-hour-a-day commitment for prayer and Bible reading is no small commitment when you are taking a full load of courses and playing basketball, too. I did little else but go to class, study, play/practice basketball, pray, read my Bible, and sleep. I realized later that God was pleased with my effort and my desire. He was perfectly willing to forgive my sins. I just wasn't aware of it at the time.

Later, one sentence from one of my seminary professors ministered great healing to me: "Remember, you can't be holy in a hurry." I thought, "Why hadn't someone told me that?" Perhaps someone had, and I just didn't hear it. Then, Psalm 103:8–14 became one of the most valued passages in all the Bible to me:

The LORD is compassionate and gracious,
Slow to anger and abounding in lovingkindness.
He will not always strive {with us};
Nor will He keep {His anger} forever.
He has not dealt with us according to our sins,
Nor rewarded us according to our iniquities.
For as high as the heavens are above the earth,
So great is His lovingkindness toward those who fear Him.
As far as the east is from the west,
So far has He removed our transgressions from us.
Just as a father has compassion on {his} children,
So the LORD has compassion on those who fear Him.
For He Himself knows our frame;
He is mindful that we are {but} dust. (NASB)

Ahh, so the Lord knows that we are but dust. How comforting. Even so, He will remove our transgressions as far from us as the east is from the west (an infinite distance). That is the message I needed to hear, and that is the message that Peter teaches us by living an imperfect life and asking Jesus the right questions. We cannot sin so many times that God will not forgive us.

Can We Sin so Badly that God Will Not Forgive Us?

We cannot sin so badly that God will not forgive Us.

Not only has Peter's life taught us that we cannot sin *so many times* that God will not forgive us, so he has also taught us that we cannot sin *so badly* that God will not forgive us. Many people have the mistaken feeling that they have committed a sin so bad that God cannot or will not forgive them. The sin varies with the one who committed it. Some feel that adultery is unforgivable, yet Jesus forgave an adulteress in the Scripture (John 8:3–11). Some believe that Jesus cannot forgive murder, yet Jesus forgave those who murdered Him ("Father, forgive them, for they do not know what they do," Luke 23:34). Someone might feel that a life of graft and extortion would be unforgivable, yet Jesus forgave Matthew and Zacchaeus of those sins (Matthew 9:9; Luke 19:1–10).

I always imagined that the greatest sin would be cursing God. Here, too, Peter comes to our rescue. Peter cursed God and denied that he ever knew Him. We read it in Matthew 26:69–74:

Now Peter was sitting outside in the courtyard, and a certain servant-girl came to him and said, "You too were with Jesus the Galilean."
But he denied it before them all, saying, "I do not know what you are talking about."
And when he had gone out to the gateway, another servant-girl saw him and said to those who were there, "This man was with Jesus of Nazareth."
And again he denied it with an oath, "I do not know the man."
And a little later the bystanders came up and said to Peter, "Surely you too are one of them; for the way you talk gives you away."
Then he began to curse and swear, "I do not know the man!" And immediately a cock crowed. (NASB)

The passage does not specifically say that he cursed God, but I have always imagined that he did, for when he denied he ever knew Him, it was with an oath, cursing and swearing. In any event, it seems to me to be the worst thing you could ever do.

Here again, we learn great things from Peter. As we read on in the account, we know that he was forgiven, for not many days later we see him eating fish with Jesus on the shore of the Sea of Galilee, in fellowship with Him. Peter demonstrated that we cannot sin so badly but that God will forgive us. I'm sorry, Peter, for your struggles. But I'm grateful for the overall message of your life.

What Is the Unpardonable Sin?

The unpardonable sin is rejecting the Holy Spirit's pull to bring us to Christ.

After saying that we cannot sin so many times but that God will forgive us, and that we cannot sin so badly but that God will forgive us, now we run headlong into what seems to be a contradiction: the unpardonable sin. The Bible does say that there is an unpardonable sin. So, what is it, and how do we reconcile it with what we have already said?

Let's read the passage in Matthew 12:22–37:

Then there was brought to Him a demon-possessed man who was blind and dumb, and He healed him, so that the dumb man spoke and saw. And all the multitudes were amazed, and began to say, "This man cannot be the Son of David, can he?"

But when the Pharisees heard it, they said, "This man casts out demons only by Beelzebub the ruler of the demons."

And knowing their thoughts He said to them, "Any kingdom divided against itself is laid waste; and any city or house divided against itself shall not stand. And if Satan casts out Satan, he is divided against himself; how then shall his kingdom stand?

"And if I by Beelzebub cast out demons, by whom do your sons cast them out? Consequently they shall be your judges. But if I cast out demons by the Spirit of God, then the kingdom of God has come upon you.

"Or how can anyone enter the strong man's house and carry off his property, unless he first binds the strong man? And then he will plunder his house.

"He who is not with Me is against Me; and he who does not gather with Me scatters.

"Therefore I say to you, any sin and blasphemy shall be forgiven men, but blasphemy against the Spirit shall not be forgiven. And whoever shall speak a word against the Son of Man, it shall be forgiven him; but whoever shall speak against the Holy Spirit, it shall not be forgiven him, either in this age, or in the age to come.

"Either make the tree good, and its fruit good; or make the tree bad, and its fruit bad; for the tree is known by its fruit.

"You brood of vipers, how can you, being evil, speak what is good? For the mouth speaks out of that which fills the heart. The good man out of his good treasure brings forth what is good; and the evil man out of his evil treasure brings forth what is evil.

"And I say to you, that every careless word that men shall speak, they shall render account for it in the day of judgment. For by your words you shall be justified, and by your words you shall be condemned." (NASB)

The key verses, of course, are 31–32, "Therefore I say to you, any sin and blasphemy shall be forgiven men, but blasphemy against the Spirit shall not be forgiven. And whoever shall speak a word against the Son of Man, it shall be forgiven him; but whoever shall speak against the Holy Spirit, it shall not be forgiven him, either in this age, or in the age to come."

Blasphemy of the Holy Spirit is the term used to describe the unpardonable sin, yet it is not simple to understand. To blaspheme means to speak impiously. On the surface, one is tempted to think that you could say something impious about Jesus and be forgiven, but if you slipped and said something impious about the Holy Spirit, you were a goner. For example, Peter swore and denied that he ever knew Jesus, and that sin was forgiven. Yet, had he slipped and sworn and denied that he ever knew the Holy Spirit, would it have sealed his doom? I think not. There is more to it than that.

We must interpret any one passage in the Bible in light of all the other passages in the Bible. The Bible never contradicts itself. Therefore, we can sometimes gain insight into an unclear passage by looking at a clear passage. John 6:37 says, "The one who comes to Me I will by no means cast out." First John 5:12 says, "He who has the Son has life." Jesus makes it clear that if *anyone* comes to Him, He will not refuse him. He makes no exceptions. Jesus also makes it clear that if anyone has the Son, he also has eternal life. So a person's eternal destiny is linked to whether or not he believes in Jesus, repents, asks Jesus to forgive him, and commits his life to Him. If a person said something impious about the Holy Spirit and then came to Jesus, Jesus would not cast him out. So merely saying something impious about the Holy Spirit is not unpardonable.

The context of the passage must tell us what it means to "blaspheme the Holy Spirit." The Pharisees knew who Jesus was, had heard His message, and had rejected Him. Because they had rejected Him, they had to explain away the miracles He was performing. If they were not of God, then the Pharisees had only one other option. His work must have been of the devil. That is why they said that Jesus cast out demons by the power of the devil.

God will only reject us when we have ultimately rejected Him.

It is the Holy Spirit's task to convict people of their sin (John 16:8) and to illumine their minds to the truth of Scripture (1 Corinthians 2:12). Unless the Holy Spirit does these things, no one can come to Christ. The Holy Spirit had convicted the Pharisees of their sin and given them reason to believe in Jesus, but because of jealousy (Mark 15:10) the Pharisees rejected the Spirit's work in their heart. This clear, calculated rejection of the work of the Holy Spirit in their lives is unpardonable, because it demonstrates their rejection of God and Jesus. No one can go to heaven who rejects Jesus. As Jesus said in Matthew 12:37, "For by your words you will be justified, and by your words you will be condemned." Their words revealed their hearts, and as long as they rejected the work of the Holy Spirit who was trying to lead them to Jesus, that sin could not be pardoned.

James Packer, in his book *Concise Theology*, writes further,

Such a sin would become unforgivable when the conscience had been so calloused by calling good evil that all sense of the moral glory of Jesus' mighty works was destroyed. This hardening of heart against Jesus would preclude any remorse at any stage for having thus blasphemed. But nonexistence of remorse makes repentance impossible, and nonexistence of repentance makes forgiveness impossible.[245]

In the *Evangelical Dictionary of Theology*, we read,

In [Jesus], in his action, God was present and active in a decisive and final way—to reject his ministry was to reject God and so too forgiveness. The [unpardonable sin] is committed when a man recognizes the mission of Jesus by the Holy Spirit but defies and resists and curses it."[2]

Another interpretation of the unpardonable sin says that the sin cannot be committed today. It could only be committed by those living at the time Jesus made His warning.

The consensus of opinion, however, is that the unpardonable sin boils down to a rejection of Jesus, who was made known to us as God through the Holy Spirit's ministry to us. That squares with all the other passages in the New Testament that talk about salvation. So, as long as there is life, there is hope that someone will turn to Christ. And if one turns to Him, Jesus will certainly not cast him out. If you are concerned about it yourself, you have not yet committed the unpardonable sin. Simply turn to Jesus as the Scriptures instruct, and you will be born again (John 3:16), and the unpardonable sin will no longer be an issue for you. You can be as relieved as I was that I not only had not committed the unpardonable sin, but could not, because I had accepted Christ as my personal savior.

Speed Bump!

Slow down to be sure you've gotten the main points of this chapter.

Question **A**nswer

Q1. Can we sin so often that God will not forgive us?

A1. We *cannot* sin so *often* that God will not forgive us.

Q2. Can we sin so badly that God will not forgive us?

A2. We *cannot* sin so *badly* that God will not forgive us.

Q3. What is the unpardonable sin?

A3. The unpardonable sin is *rejecting* the Holy Spirit's pull to bring us to Christ.

Fill in the Blank

Question **A**nswer

Q1. Can we sin so often that God will not forgive us?

A1. We _____ sin so _____ that God will not forgive us.

Q2. Can we sin so badly that God will not forgive us?

A2. We _____ sin so _____ that God will not forgive us.

Q3. What is the unpardonable sin?

A3. The unpardonable sin is _____ the Holy Spirit's pull to bring us to Christ.

For Further Thought and Discussion

1. Have you ever feared that you had committed the unpardonable sin? If so, has this chapter given you any new information? If you need to, why not accept Christ right now, and put the issue behind you?

2. Have you ever feared that, as a Christian, you had sinned so badly that Christ would not forgive you? If so, has this chapter given you any new information? Accept Christ's invitation to full forgiveness.

3. Have you ever feared that, as a Christian, you had sinned so often that Christ would not forgive you? If so, has this chapter given you any new information? Accept Christ's invitation to full forgiveness.

What If I Don't Believe?

If I don't believe that I cannot sin so badly or so often but that Christ will forgive me, I may go through great agony of spirit, great torment, and great fear of death. I am rejecting the teaching of Scripture as well as the example of Peter. We cannot do anything to make God love us more, and we cannot do anything to make God love us less. The only unforgivable sin is finally and irrevocably refusing to accept Jesus as our savior, and dying in that condition.

For Further Study

1. Scripture

- Psalm 103:8–14

- Matthew 18:21–35

- Matthew 26:69–74

- Luke 23:34

2. Books

Several other books are very helpful in studying this subject further. They are listed below in general order of difficulty.

Grace Awakening, Charles Swindoll
Forgiveness, Charles Stanley
Eternal Security, Charles Stanley

*When Christians meet . . . to take counsel
together, their purpose is not—or should not
be—to ascertain what is the mind of the
majority, but what is the mind of the Holy
Spirit—something which may be quite
different.*
■ Margaret Thatcher (former Prime Minister
of Great Britain)

How Do I Respond to the Holy Spirit?

A friend of mine once went on a fast for health reasons. It was going to be a one-week fast, drinking only water and juices. He was a very large man, and the fast didn't go well. The first day, he was hungry. The second day, he was very hungry. The third day he was ravenous. On the fourth day, he was out mowing his yard, trying to do something constructive to keep his mind occupied and off thoughts of "food." However, when you are really hungry, only food will do. It was early in the spring, and an asparagus patch was just peeking its head above the surface of the ground. He was trimming up around the trees, bushes, and sidewalk when he came to the asparagus patch. Whether it was because his hunger exploded at that precise moment, or whether the asparagus, being a reasonable approximation of food, triggered something deep within him, he cracked. He dropped to his knees and began plucking off handfuls of the tender shoots. Then my friend, who had never been fond of asparagus in any form, began eating the raw aparagus, stuffing it wildly into his mouth like some savage. Appetite unabated, he ran, chewing and stumbling, toward the house, leaving the lawnmower running. He crashed through the kitchen door, threw a hamburger in a skillet, made a sandwich, and took several big bites. As I said, when you are hungry, only food will do.

Many people today are spiritually hungry. They are hungry for a sense of intimacy with God, hungry for a sense of meaning and purpose in life, and hungry for a feeling of power or control over the negative things in life. Unfortunately some are grabbing wildly at fringe religions, mindless emotions, and New Age ideas, stuffing these indiscriminately into their spiritual mouths. On the other hand, for many there is a renewed interest in the Holy Spirit. This is the right decision, because the Holy Spirit has the answers to many of our felt needs.

In this chapter we learn that . . .

1. We grieve the Holy Spirit when we choose, knowingly and willingly, to sin.
2. We quench the Spirit when we fail to yield to His leading in our lives.
3. We walk in the Spirit when we consciously and prayerfully focus on the potential of the Holy Spirit's convicting, illuminating, leading, or enabling ministry coming to us at any moment, and keep ourselves prepared to follow and obey.

Concerning intimacy with God, for which many of us long, we read,

"Now we have received, not the spirit of the world, but the Spirit who is from God, that we might know the things that have been freely given to us by God. These things we also speak, not in words which man's wisdom teaches but which the Holy Spirit teaches, comparing spiritual things with spiritual. . . . We have the mind of Christ" (1 Corinthians 2:12–13, 16).

What greater intimacy could we have than to know the things of God, freely given to us by God through the Holy Spirit, and to have the mind of Christ?

Concerning meaning and purpose in life, we read, "Do you not know that your body is the temple of the Holy Spirit who is in you, whom you have from God, and you are not your own? For you were bought at a price; therefore glorify God in your body and in your spirit, which are God's" (1 Corinthians 6:19–20).

What greater purpose could we have than to be a dwelling place of God, and to bring glory to Him?

Concerning power, we read, "Now may the God of hope fill you with all joy and peace in believing, that you may abound in hope by the power of the Holy Spirit" (Romans 15:13).

What greater power could we have than to be filled with hope and joy and peace by the power of the Holy Spirit?

Yes, we are right to turn to the Holy Spirit to fill our spiritual hunger for intimacy with God, for purpose, and for power, for those are His ministries to God's children. But how do we experience the ministry of the Holy Spirit in our lives?

Let us be perfectly clear on one thing. The Holy Spirit is not called the Happy Spirit. He is not called the Self-Fulfilled Spirit. He is not called the Easy-Going Spirit. He is called the *Holy* Spirit for a reason. His primary focus is holiness, and when the Holy Spirit works in your life, He has one primary goal: your holiness. Unless we remember this we will misunderstand His work in our lives. We will misinterpret His strategy and methodology. We will misperceive His love, care, and concern for us. The Holy Spirit feels free to ask us to give up whatever is necessary in the pursuit of holiness. As a result, the road to holiness is not always smooth, level, or easy. The journey may be difficult, but the destination is priceless.

Why I need to know this

I need to know how to respond to the Holy Spirit so I will avoid the trap of living as though He had no role to play in my life. I would become a functional agnostic, living as though truth did not even exist. I would have diminished power to live as I ought, and diminished satisfaction with my life as a Christian and my relationship with God, to say nothing of the fact that my life would not be pleasing to Him.

There are, then, positive and negative ways in which we must respond to the Holy Spirit. That is, there are things we must do, and there are things we must not do as we pursue intimacy with God through the Holy Spirit.

What Does It Mean to Grieve the Holy Spirit?

We grieve the Holy Spirit when we choose, knowingly and willingly, to sin.

Central Passage: Ephesians 4:30, "Do not grieve the Holy Spirit of God, by whom you were sealed for the day of redemption."

Anyone with any age and experience has been grieved by the self-destructive behavior of loved ones. It drives an invisible knife into our hearts to see them make foolish or carnal or self-destructive decisions. It may be a daughter who marries a man who is not worthy of her, or a son who is hooked on alcohol or cocaine. Perhaps a brother, sister, or friend loses a good job because of dishonesty. Their behavior brings us inner pain.

In the same way, we can grieve the Holy Spirit. In Ephesians 4:30, we read, "Do not grieve the Holy Spirit of God, by whom you were sealed for the day of redemption." The Holy Spirit instructs us (1 John 2:27), illumines our minds to the truth of Scripture (1 Corinthians 2:12–13), convicts us of sin (John 16:8), and leads us in righteousness (Romans 8:14). It is the Holy Spirit who lives within us and tries to get us to live lives of holy service to God. When we disobey His instruction to us, it grieves Him. When He illumines our mind to the truth of a Scripture and we fail to obey, it grieves Him. When He convicts us of sin and tries to get us to turn from sin, and we resist and rebuff Him, it grieves Him. It hurts Him much as it hurts us when someone we love wallows in self-destructive behavior. Our first step in responding to the Holy Spirit is to avoid grieving Him—to not disobey Him when He convicts us of sin.

What Does It Mean to Quench the Holy Spirit?

We quench the Spirit when we fail to yield to His leading in our lives.

Central Passage: 1 Thessalonians 5:19, *Do not quench the Spirit.*

To quench means to stifle or extinguish. First Thessalonians 5:19 commands us, "Do not quench the Spirit." Of course, we cannot extinguish the Holy Spirit as a divine being, but we can extinguish His work in our lives by refusing to respond to or cooperate with His work in our lives. Philippians 2:12–13 says, "Work out your own salvation with fear and trembling; for it is God who works in you both to will and to do for His good pleasure."

The Holy Spirit, in addition to convicting us of sin, also supernaturally helps us understand the Bible, leads us, and guides us. The Holy Spirit places a thought or urging or conviction or sense of "ought-ness" in our minds to do something good and right. When we respond in faith and obedience to this work of God, then we are strengthened, spiritually enlarged, enlightened, and increased in our capacity to respond to something even greater next time. That is honoring the Holy Spirit. When we ignore His leading, or procrastinate, or make excuses, or simply disobey, that quenches the Holy Spirit. In addition, we are weakened, spiritually diminished, darkened in our understanding, and decreased in our capacity to respond to something even greater next time. That is dishonoring the Holy Spirit. The second step in responding to the Holy Spirit is to not quench Him—to not fail to yield our lives to His leading.

What Does It Mean to Walk in the Spirit?

We walk in the Spirit when we consciously and prayerfully focus on the potential of the Holy Spirit's convicting, illuminating, leading, or enabling ministry coming to us at any moment, and keep ourselves prepared to follow and obey.

Central Passage: Galatians 5:16, *Walk in the Spirit, and you shall not fulfill the lust of the flesh.*

There is no common agreement in Christendom as to what it means to walk in the Spirit, except on some very broad parameters. Therefore, I will try to stick with those parameters. To walk in the Spirit must surely include something very close to trusting and obeying Christ, for the demands and the results are the same. We find that we are promised joy and peace through the Holy Spirit ("Now may the God of hope fill you with all joy and peace in believing, that you may abound in hope by the power of the Holy Spirit," Romans 15:13), and yet the same things are promised to us through Jesus ("These things I have spoken to you, that My joy may remain in you, and that your joy may be full," John 15:11; "Peace I leave with you, My peace I give to you; not as the world gives do I give to you. Let not your heart be troubled, neither let it be afraid," John 14:27).

Yet there is a valid focus on walking in the Spirit that is distinct from, though not divorced from, trusting and obeying Christ. To understand the Holy Spirit's ministry, and what we must do to walk in the Spirit, we must remember that the purpose of the Spirit's ministry is to glorify Christ. On the night of His betrayal Jesus said of the Spirit that "He will glorify me," and that the purpose of the Spirit's ministry is to "take of what is Mine [Jesus'] and declare it to you" (John 16:14). In other words, the Holy Spirit will cause Jesus to be glorious in people's eyes. He will make them aware of the glory that Jesus had already and that would be enhanced even more when He returned to heaven.

The purpose of the Holy Spirit is to glorify Christ.

No understanding of the Holy Spirit is complete without understanding that the Father's purpose is that the Son be known, loved, honored, praised, worshiped, and made preeminent in everything, and that the Spirit's role is to make sure that happens. To focus on the Spirit in a way that causes us to overlook Christ is a mistake that contradicts the basic work of the Spirit.

Step 1: Repenting of Sin

The will of God for us is our sanctification, our being set apart for His fellowship and His service. That means that the first step in walking in the Spirit is consciously and prayerfully focusing on the Holy Spirit's convicting ministry in our lives, living in a state of preparedness to repent. As the Holy Spirit convicts us of sin in our lives (makes our sin known to us), we must repent, or turn around. Since we are imperfect and immature beings, repentance could be defined as "turning from as much as you know of your sin to give as much as you know of yourself to as much as you know of God," and as your knowledge and maturity grow, your capacity to repent grows. Everything the Christian is and does must be seen in light of one overriding fact: He belongs to Christ and has been separated from everything and everyone in creation in order to belong to his God alone. Again, as Packer writes "Ordered, costly, unstinting commitment for the Lord's sake to spouse, children, parents, employers, employees, and all one's other neighbors, on the basis of being radically detached from them all to belong to God—Father, Son and Spirit—and to no one else, is the unvarying shape of the authentically holy life" (*Keep in Step with the Spirit* 105).

Step 2: Responding to Truth

Our second step in walking in the Spirit is focusing on the potential of the Holy Spirit to illumine our minds to a truth of Scripture and living in a state of preparedness to follow and obey. The illuminating ministry of the Spirit is that supernatural work in which He enables us to understand the spiritual truths of the Scripture and their application to our lives (1 Corinthians 2:11–16). It may be in a quiet time of personal devotion or in the hubbub of life that the Scripture comes alive to us. We understand it, or we understand how it applies to us in a given situation. We see the truth, the way. It now remains for us to walk in the truth we now understand. When we do, we are walking in the Spirit, for the Spirit enabled us to understand the truth of Scripture. When we don't, we are grieving the Holy Spirit; for we know what we should do and we don't do it. That is sin (Romans 14:23).

Step 3: Following His Leading

The third element of walking in the Spirit is consciously and prayerfully focusing on the potential of the Holy Spirit's leading in our lives and keeping ourselves prepared to follow. This is a little more tricky, because we must discern whether or not something is the "leading of the Lord" before we are obligated to follow it. We do this by searching the Scripture, prayer, counsel from friends, assessment of circumstances, and so forth. However, to be frank, sometimes the leading of the Lord comes in quick, seemingly insignificant spurs of the moment, to do something good for someone. My pastor in seminary used to say, "Follow your good impulses. It is probably the Holy Spirit." I always took that as good advice. You don't have to make a pro and con list and meditate on it for twenty-four hours if the impulse comes to you to say something encouraging and kind to someone. Often the Spirit ministers through us powerfully when we obey such impulses. If the matter is something transparently good, and must be done right away or the opportunity will be lost, you are pretty safe to go ahead and do it. The bigger things, of course, require more attention.

Step 4: Doing His Work

The fourth element of walking in the Spirit is consciously and prayerfully focusing on the potential for the Holy Spirit's enabling ministry to come to us at any moment and keeping ourselves prepared to follow and obey. This is very similar to the Spirit's leading, but often we may fear we are not able to do something we think God may be asking of us. Of course, God will never ask anything of us that we cannot do, but prudence sometimes demands that we think something through before jumping off the high dive. On the other hand, the Holy Spirit may have clearly gifted us for a certain ministry and we need to be ready to minister, knowing that He has enabled us. Or, He may choose to use us in a totally new way, so we must be ready to consider that possibility and obey if it becomes evident that God is leading us.

Conclusion

So many of us long for power—power to withstand the trials of life, or power to be effective in service to God. We long for power to bring meaning to our lives, to reassure us that we matter to God and that He is, in fact, using us. We long for power to overcome the sin and the habits and the weaknesses that drag us down in our pursuit of a meaningful relationship with the Lord. In the pursuit of these legitimate longings, we often look to satisfy them through quick fixes rather than a consistent commitment to Jesus and His holiness.

When you look up "power" in an English Bible concordance, you will find that occurrences of "power" after the book of Acts usually do not refer to things we would ordinarily call miraculous. They more commonly link with the subtle but powerful things of the deeper inner life. For example, we see God's power revealed in the life of individual Christians in ways that we usually think of as common, everyday. Yet if the Bible is true, the common and everyday in the Christian life are also miraculous and powerful. And, when you think of such "mere" Christian living done consistently, we see it more clearly for what it is . . . true, spiritual power.

1. Power to experience joy, peace and hope: "Now may the God of hope fill you with all joy and peace in believing, that you may abound in hope by the power of the Holy Spirit" (Romans 15:13).

2. Power to be saved from our sins: "For the message of the cross is foolishness to those who are perishing, but to us who are being saved it is the power of God" (1 Corinthians 1:18).

3. Power to endure affliction: "And He said to me, 'My grace is sufficient for you, for My strength is made perfect in weakness.' Therefore most gladly I will rather boast in my infirmities, that the power of Christ may rest upon me" (2 Corinthians 12:9).

4. Power to minister to others: "I became a minister [of the gospel] according to the gift of the grace of God given to me by the effective working of His power" (Ephesians 3:7).

5. Power to be rooted and grounded in love, to comprehend

the love of Christ, and to be filled up to all the fullness of God: "For this reason I bow my knees to the Father of our Lord Jesus Christ, from whom the whole family in heaven and earth is named, that He would grant you, according to the riches of His glory, to be strengthened with might [power] through His Spirit in the inner man, that Christ may dwell in your hearts through faith; [and] that you, being rooted and grounded in love, may be able to comprehend with all the saints what is the width and length and depth and height—to know the love of Christ which passes knowledge, that you may be filled with all the fullness of God" (Ephesians 3:14–19).

6. Power to be steadfast and patient, and thankful: "For this reason we also, since the day we heard it, do not cease to pray for you, and to ask that you may be filled with the knowledge of His will in all wisdom and spiritual understanding; that you may walk worthy of the Lord, fully pleasing Him, being fruitful in every good work and increasing in the knowledge of God; strengthened with all might, according to His glorious power, for all patience and longsuffering with joy; giving thanks to the Father who has qualified us to be partakers of the inheritance of the saints in the light" (Colossians 1:9–12).

7. Power to proclaim and teach Christ: "And we proclaim Him, admonishing every man and teaching every man with all wisdom, that we may present every man complete in Christ. And for this purpose also I labor, striving according to His power, which mightily works within me" (Colossians 1:28–29, NASB).

8. Power to be bold and to suffer: "For God has not given us a spirit of fear, but of power and love and of a sound mind. Therefore do not be ashamed of the testimony of our Lord, nor of me His prisoner, but share with me in the sufferings for the gospel according to the power of God" (2 Timothy 1:7–8).

We may not all be able to witness fireballs from heaven, but we all can witness this subtle but miraculous power in our lives as we live in dependence on Him, walking in His Spirit.

God does the work of God, and Man does the work of Man. Man can't do the work of God, and God won't do the work of Man. I use "Man" in the generic sense of "humanity." Therefore, we must be clear on what the work of God is and what our work is and make sure we are doing our job and not trying to do God's. We have a genius for turning things around. We often insist on trying to do the work of God while neglecting the work of Man.

God expects things from us. He works through the things we do, such as Bible study, prayer, fellowship with other Christians, worship, the Lord's Supper, as well as the more subjective things like reflection, self-examination, sharing with others, and so forth.

Again, Packer writes,

> The Spirit shows His power to us, not by constantly interrupting our use of these [disciplines] with visions, impressions, or prophecies, which serve up to us ready-made insights on a plate, so to speak, but rather by making these regular means effective to change us for the better and for the wiser as we go along. Holiness teaching that skips over disciplined persistence in the well-doing that forms holy habits is thus weak; habit forming is the Spirit's ordinary way of leading us on in holiness. These habits, once won, must not be seen as the result of self effort. Without the blessing and energizing and overseeing ministry of the Holy Spirit, we would not be able to sustain them, nor would they reap their spiritual fruit (*Keep in Step with the Spirit* 109)

Twice Paul speaks of being "led" by the Spirit (Romans 8:14; Galatians 5:18). Both times the guidance is not a revealing to our minds of divine directives hitherto unknown; it is, rather, an impelling of our wills to pursue and practice and hold fast that sanctity whose terms we know already. Thus to be led and guided, says Paul, is the mark of a Christian (118).

To be led by the Spirit is the mark of a Christian.

A. J. Gordon, one of the founders of Gordon-Conwell Divinity School, told of being out walking and looking across a field at a house. There beside the house was what looked like a man pumping furiously at one of those hand pumps. As Gordon watched, the man continued to pump at a tremendous rate; he seemed absolutely tireless, pumping on and on, up and down, without ever slowing in the slightest, much less stopping.

Truly it was a remarkable sight, so Gordon started to walk toward it. As he got closer, he could see it was not a man at the pump, but a wooden figure painted to look like a man. The arm that was pumping so rapidly was hinged at the elbow and the hand was wired to the pump handle. The water was pouring forth, but not because the figure was pumping it. You see, it was an artesian well, and the water was pumping the man!

When you see a man who is at work for God and proucing

results, recognize that it is the Holy Spirit working through him, not the man's efforts that are giving results. All he has to do is keep his hand on the handle. The handle, of course, is the Holy Spirit, and you keep your hand on the handle through all the things we talked about in this chapter.

Speed Bump!
Slow down to be sure you've gotten the main points of this chapter.

Question **A**nswer

Q1. What does it mean to grieve the Holy Spirit?

A1. We grieve the Holy Spirit when we choose, knowingly and willingly, to *sin.*

Q2. What does it mean to quench the Holy Spirit?

A2. We quench the Spirit when we fail to *yield* to His leading in our lives.

Q3. What does it mean to walk in the Spirit?

A3. We walk in the Spirit when we consciously and prayerfully focus on the potential of the Holy Spirit's convicting, illuminating, leading, or enabling ministry coming to us at any moment, and keep ourselves *prepared* to follow and obey.

Fill in the Blank

Question **A**nswer

Q1. What does it mean to grieve the Holy Spirit?

A1. We grieve the Holy Spirit when we choose, knowingly and willingly, to _____.

Q2. What does it mean to quench the Holy Spirit?

A2. We quench the Spirit when we fail to _____ to His leading in our lives.

Q3. What does it mean to walk in the Spirit?

A3. We walk in the Spirit when we consciously and prayerfully focus on the potential of the Holy Spirit's convicting, illuminating, leading, or enabling ministry coming to us at any moment, and keep ourselves _____ to follow and obey.

For Further Thought and Discussion

1. What are some instances when you have grieved the Holy Spirit? Are there things you need to repent of right now and stop grieving the Holy Spirit? What is the greatest factor encouraging you to grieve the Holy Spirit?

2. What are some examples of times you have quenched the Holy Spirit by not following His leading? Is there anything right now that you need to do to stop quenching Him? What is the greatest factor encouraging you to quench the Holy Spirit?

3. We looked at four parts to walking in the Spirit: repenting of sin, responding to biblical truth, following His leading, and doing His work. Which of these areas is your greatest need? Which one is your greatest strength? What else do you need to be doing right now to walk in the Spirit?

What If I Don't Believe?

If I don't believe how I must respond to the Holy Spirit, I stand the very real chance of living a frustrated and ineffective Christian life. I must understand that I can grieve the Holy Spirit or quench His work in my life, and that I must walk in the Spirit, not "fulfill the lusts of the flesh."

For Further Study

1. Scripture

- John 16:8
- Romans 8:14
- 1 Corinthians 2:11–16
- Galatians 5:16–23
- Ephesians 4:30
- 1 Thessalonians 5:19
- 1 John 2:27

2. Books

Several other books are very helpful in studying this subject. They are listed below in general order of difficulty. If I could read only one of these, I would read the first one.

The Holy Spirit, Billy Graham
Keep in Step With the Spirit, James I. Packer
True Spirituality, Francis Schaeffer

> *I've never known a person whom I thought was truly filled with the Holy Spirit who went out and bragged about it or sought to draw attention to himself.*
> ■ **Billy Graham**

What Is the Fruit of the Spirit? (Part One)

In the early part of our marriage, my wife and I lived for a year in Portland, Oregon. We bought a modest little home in an older part of town, and as we began to settle in, I noticed a fruit tree in the corner of our front yard. I didn't know what kind of fruit tree it was—just that it was a fruit tree. As winter turned to spring, and spring to summer, I learned that we had a plum tree. The white blossoms turned into little green marbles that lengthened, grew, and ripened into glorious green plums (yes, green!). As they ripened, we tasted them cautiously and discovered that they were sweet and delicious. They had no bugs or worms, even though we had not sprayed them, and when my mother came to visit, she canned so many jars of plum jelly that we ate it for years afterward.

I grew up in rural north central Indiana, not far from the golden dome of the University of Notre Dame. As a country boy, I knew just a little about trees. For example, I knew if a tree was an oak, or a maple, or a fruit tree, but I didn't know what kind of an oak (red or white), what kind of maple (silver or sugar), or what kind of fruit tree (apple, cherry, or peach). I have always liked fruit trees. They all tend to have a delicate, parchment-like bark, pointed, oblong leaves, and beautiful white or pink flowers in the spring. But as with the plum tree, I always had to wait until it bore fruit to be sure of its type.

People are a lot like that. They are all quite similar in many respects, but you never really know what kind of person one is until he or she begins to produce fruit. Everyone bears fruit. It may be good fruit or wormy fruit, sweet fruit or sour fruit, abundant fruit or meager fruit; but we all bear fruit. And everyone around us eventually knows what kind of fruit tree we are. It cannot be hidden.

Our fruit is revealed both by what we do and by what we don't do. It is revealed by what we say and what we don't say. It is revealed even by what we laugh at or don't laugh at. We cannot help but reveal who we are. It is embarrassing when you finally realize that you hide nothing from others. We pretend we do, and others pretend not to notice. But sooner or later we reveal who we really are. We bear our fruit.

In this chapter we learn that . . .

1. The fruit of the Spirit are character qualities God possesses and that the Holy Spirit imparts to us as we live in trusting obedience to Jesus.
2. Love is the steady direction of our will toward the lasting good of another.
3. Joy is a deep sense of well-being that is not dependent upon favorable circumstances, but rooted in a fundamental acceptance of, and confidence in, the will of God.
4. Peace is the absence of anxiety and the presence of trusting assurance in the promises of God.

In the book of Galatians, the Bible presents a stark contrast between two kinds of fruit: the fruit of the flesh and the fruit of the Spirit. We see the fruit of the flesh in 5:19–21: "Now the works of the flesh are evident, which are: adultery, fornication, uncleanness, lewdness, idolatry, sorcery, hatred, contentions, jealousies, outbursts of wrath, selfish ambitions, dissensions, heresies, envy, murders, drunkenness, revelries, and the like." Whew! What a list! It's like a verbal snapshot inside the hearts of Attila the Hun, Genghis Khan, and Adolf Hitler, all rolled into one.

"But the fruit of the Spirit is love, joy, peace, patience, kindness, goodness, faithfulness, gentleness, self-control" (5:22–23, NASB). Ah, what a list! It is like a verbal snapshot inside the heart of God!

When we allow our base desires to rule our lives, we get the first list. When we allow the Holy Spirit to rule our lives, we get the second list. In America today, we are trying to get the second list by indulging in the first. We are trying to get peace, love, and joy by committing adultery and fornication, pursuing selfish ambition, and enjoying drunken revelries. It won't work, however. You can only reap what you sow. You must sow obedience to and reliance upon the Holy Spirit if you are to reap His fruit.

What Is the Fruit of the Spirit?

The fruit of the Spirit are character qualities that God possesses and that the Holy Spirit imparts to us as we live in trusting obedience to Jesus.

The description of the fruit of the Spirit has a very logical place in the argument of the book of Galatians. The apostle Paul is arguing that there are two ways to live the Christian life. One is by obeying a long set of dos and don'ts. The other is by walking by the Spirit. Paul is saying that these believers should not resort to rule-keeping—even if the rules are the great Law of Moses. Instead, they should respond to the leading and direction of the Holy Spirit. Whenever people do, they begin to experience the fruit of the Holy Spirit. When they don't, they experience the fruit of the flesh.

The law puts the believer into bondage. The Spirit gives the believer freedom. Paul's appeal is to "Stand fast therefore in the liberty by which Christ has made us free, and do not be entangled again with a yoke of bondage" (Galatians 5:1).

Why I need to know this

If I don't know that the fruit of the Spirit are character qualities that God possesses and that He wants me to possess, I may miss out on the spiritual growth and personal transformation God intends for me. Unless I realize that they are the fruit of the Spirit rather than mere self-effort, I might become unduly frustrated when my self-effort does not produce the results I want to see in my life. I must know about the fruit and cooperate with God in the process of acquiring the fruit, but rely and trust in Him for the appearance of the fruit in my life.

The fruit of the Spirit, then, is our focus and goal. When we read over that marvelous list, who would not want those qualities to characterize his life? Who doesn't want peace, love, and joy? Who doesn't want to be patient, kind, and good? It would take a hard heart to turn that down. But often we don't want to pay the price to gain them. Too often, we want to "sow to the flesh" and reap the Spirit. It doesn't work.

Nine qualities embody the fruit of the Spirit, and in Billy Graham's book *The Holy Spirit*, he observes that these nine fruit are divided into three clusters of three.

Love, joy, and peace make up the first cluster. They especially speak of our Godward relationship. The second "cluster"—patience, kindness and goodness—especially is seen in our manward relationship, that is, our relationship with other people. The third "cluster" of faithfulness, gentleness and self-control is especially seen in our inward relationship—the attitudes and actions of the inner self.

At the same time, of course, these three "clusters" are all related to each other, and all should characterize our lives. And all will characterize our lives when we abide in Christ and allow the Holy Spirit to do His work in us (187).

This statement not only helps break down the subject for more in-depth study, but it also makes it easier to memorize the fruit of the Spirit.

What Is Love?

Love is the steady direction of our will toward the lasting good of another.

I consider *Ben Hur* one of the greatest stories ever written. General Lew Wallace was an unbelieving Civil War general who, after the war, decided to write a book to discredit Christianity. After intense personal study, he became a Christian; and instead of writing a book to discredit Christianity, wrote one to reveal to the world who Christ really was, the Son of God.

The story is also a story of profound human love. Judah Ben Hur was a young, wealthy nobleman in Jerusalem, falsely accused of trying to kill the new Roman governor. Without trial, he was sent as a slave to row in the belly of a military ship. No one ever survived the slave ships. His mother and sister were arrested and sent to prison, which was little better than a slave ship. Few survived for long in those dark, dank, rat-infested, disease-ridden tombs for the living.

All seemed hopeless, yet one thought possessed Judah, drove him, and forced him to live: somehow he had to get home to Jerusalem to free his mother and sister from prison.

Opportunity began to unfold when his ship was damaged in a battle and began sinking; Judah saved the commander of the fleet from drowning. As a reward, he was taken to Rome and given his freedom. From there he made his way to Jerusalem, only to learn that his mother and sister had contracted leprosy in prison and were now existing as "living dead" in a leper colony outside the city. The most feared disease of the ancient world had turned them into monsters, with disfigured faces, and stumps where their hands and feet should have been. Because it was a contagious disease, all lepers were required to live apart from the rest of society.

Throwing aside concern for his own well-being, Judah went to the leper colony and, in a tender and moving gesture, took his mother and sister in his arms and removed them from the colony. This was the moral equivalent of taking on himself the disease that was mutilating his loved ones, since he knew he could easily contract the disease from them. At the urging of a friend, he took them to Jesus, but unfortunately, just in time to see Him crucified. They thought all hope was lost; but as the sky turned dark, lightning flashed, thunder rolled, and earthquakes shook, Judah's mother and sister were cleansed of their leprosy through faith in Jesus.

Now, I haven't forgotten that this is fiction. This story did not happen, but it still contains a great truth. Judah's love for his mother and sister compelled him to give of what he had for the need of another. No price was too great to save his loved ones if he could.

Love gives of itself for another.

We cannot, of course, love everyone with that degree of sacrifice. We can only be in one place at a time. But this story shows us a little of what love is. Love gives of itself for the needs of another.

First Corinthians 13:4–7 describes the kind of love God wants to guide our lives:

> Love is patient, love is kind, and is not jealous; love does not brag and is not arrogant, does not act unbecomingly; it does not seek its own, is not provoked, does not take into account a wrong suffered, does not rejoice in unrighteousness, but rejoices with the truth; bears all things, believes all things, hopes all things, endures all things. (NASB)

This, of course, is the kind of love He demonstrated toward us. In spite of my sin, when all of my sins were in the future, Christ died for my sins. He went to the cross so that I would not have to suffer eternal separation from God. Romans 5:8 says that God demonstrated His love toward us, in that, "while we were still sinners, Christ died for us."

Christ knew the worst about us, but He still died and then held out His hand to us and said, "Come to me, and I will give you eternal life." That kind of love is difficult to fathom, yet it is the kind of love that God calls us to live out. He promised us that kind of capacity when He said that the fruit of the Spirit is love. We can have that kind of love.

God calls us to Christlike love.

In fact, love is to be the mark of a Christian. The apostle John recorded Jesus' words, "By this all will know that you are My disciples, if you have love for one another" (John 13:35). Again, John wrote, "We know that we have passed from death to life, because we love the brethren [fellow Christians]" (1 John 3:14). The apostle Paul wrote, "Owe nothing to anyone except to love one another; for he who loves his neighbor has fulfilled the law" (Romans 13:8, NASB).

No matter what else we might say or do, if we do not have love, our life is a failure. Love is greater than any other characteristic, word, or deed. Again, the apostle Paul wrote, "If I speak with the tongues of men and of angels, but do not have love, I have become a noisy gong or a clanging cymbal. And if I have the gift of prophecy, and know all mysteries and all knowledge; and if I have all faith, so as to remove mountains, but do not have love, I am nothing. And if I give all my possessions to feed the poor, and if I deliver my body to be burned, but do not have love, it profits me nothing" (1 Corinthians 13:1–3, NASB).

Francis Schaeffer, an evangelical theologian, has even gone so far as to say that love was the "badge" of a Christian. Not only does the apostle John say that if we love one another, we demonstrate to the world that we are Christ's disciples, but also that this love would produce unity. In John 17:21, Jesus prayed to the Father that "they [Christians] all may be one, as You, Father, are in Me, and I in You; that they also may be one in Us, that the world may believe that You sent Me."

Love is the Christian's badge of identity.

Therefore, Schaeffer reasoned, if the world does not see us loving one another and living in unity, then the world has reason to believe that we are not Christ's disciples, and that Jesus was not sent from God. Interestingly enough, in a survey a number of years ago the two most important reasons non-Christians gave for not being Christians were (1) all the hypocrites in the church, and (2) they didn't believe that Jesus was God. Interesting correlation!

This helps us grasp the phenomenal importance of living in love. It is no accident, I think, that love is mentioned first in the fruit of the Spirit. Paul wrote in 1 Corinthians 13:13, "Now abide faith, hope, love, these three; but the greatest of these is love."

C. S. Lewis wrote a small book entitled *The Four Loves* that may help us understand the kind of love that is a fruit of the Spirit. Lewis was a brilliant scholar in literature who taught at Oxford and Cambridge Universities. He was also a devout Christian and applied his profound intellect to helping make Christianity more understandable. There are four words in Greek, the original language of the New Testament, that are all translated into English as "love." They are *eros*, meaning physical love; *philos*, meaning the love of friendship; *storge*, meaning family love; and *agape*, meaning divine love.

When the Bible describes God's love for us, and the love that He wants and even commands us to have, the word used is *agape* (pronounced uh-gop'-ay). This word was virtually unknown in the ancient world, because it was so foreign to human behavior. When Matthew recorded the words of Jesus when He said, "Love your enemies," he used *agape*. When John recorded Jesus' words to love one another, he used *agape*. When Mark recorded Jesus' words, "You shall love your neighbor," he used *agape*.

God's love acts—it gives.

Today, love is usually understood to be an emotion or feeling. There can be emotion associated with *agape*, but it is much more than that, as we see from the descriptions of the word in the Bible. "Love," said Bishop Neill, "is the steady direction of the will toward another's lasting good" (*The Christian Character* 22). *Agape* love acts, does, gives. When the Bible said, "For God so loved the world that He gave His only begotten Son" (John 3:16), it did not mean that goose pimples ran up and down God's spine when He looked at humanity. Rather, it meant that God was prepared to direct His will toward our lasting good.

What Is Joy?

Joy is a deep sense of well-being that is not dependent upon favorable circumstances, but rooted in a fundamental acceptance of, and confidence in, the will of God.

I mentioned Corrie ten Boom earlier who was imprisoned in a Nazi concentration camp for helping Jews escape Nazi persecution. The suffering she experienced was beyond description, and she told her story in the remarkable book, *The Hiding Place*. After she was providentially released from the concentration camp, she traveled all over the world with the message that the light of Jesus is greater than the darkness of any sin. Her post-concentration camp story is told in a number of different books, including *Tramp for the Lord*. In this latter book, she told of going to a prison in Rwanda, Africa, which was one of the worst she had ever seen. Prisoners lived in squalor, sat in steaming mud in the open air, and wore masks of despair, hopelessness and anger.

"What could I, an old Dutch woman, say to these miserable men that would help their lives?" I wondered.

"Lord," I prayed, "I am not able to overcome this darkness."

"Take My promise of Galatians 5:22," I heard an inner voice say.

Quickly I took my Bible and opened it to that passage. "But the fruit of the Spirit is love. . . ."

"Thank you, Lord," I whispered. "But I have a great love for these men already or I would not be here."

I read on. "But the fruit of the Spirit is love, joy. . . ."

"Joy?" I asked. "In these surroundings?" Then I remembered what Nehemiah said, "The joy of the Lord is my strength."

"Yes, Lord," I cried out. "That is what I need. That is what I claim. I claim the promise of joy."

I began to talk of the joy that is ours when we know Jesus. What a Friend we have in Him. He is always with us. When we are depressed, He gives us joy. When we do wrong, He gives us the strength to be good. When we hate, He fills us with His forgiveness. When we are afraid, He causes us to love.

Several faces changed and I saw that some of my joy was spilling over on them. But I knew what the rest were thinking: *After your talk you can go home, away from this muddy, stinking prison. It is easy to talk about joy when you are free. But we must stay here.*

Then she told them her story of the hardship, deprivation and suffering she experienced in the concentration camp. The hunger, the dehumanization, the lack of sleep, standing in line for hours outside as the icy-cold wind ripped through them, the lack of medical attention, the disease. One morning during roll call a woman collapsed.

In a moment a young woman guard was standing over her, a whip in her hand, screaming in rage, "Get up. How dare you think you can lie down when everyone else is standing?"

I looked out at the men who were sitting in front of me. No longer were their faces filled with darkness and anger. They were listening—intently—for they were hearing from someone who had walked where they were now walking.

"Say, men," I said, "do you know Jesus is willing to live in your hearts? He says 'I stand at the door of your heart and knock. If anyone hears my voice and opens the door, I come in.' Just think: that same Jesus loves you and will live in your heart and give you joy in the midst of all this mud. He who is willing, raise his hand."

I looked around. All the men, including the guards, had raised their hands. It was unbelievable, but their faces showed a joy that only the Holy Spirit could produce.

A missionary turned to her as they drove away later.

"I must confess to you that I thought this place was too dark for the light of the Gospel. I had been here once before and was so frightened I said I would never come back. Now . . . I have seen what the Holy Spirit can do. The joy of the Lord is available, even for such a place as this. From now on I shall return every week to tell them about Jesus."

Months later I received a letter from her in which she said, "The fear is gone. The joy remains" (*Tramp for the Lord* 81–82).

Joy is an illusive thing. The world knows almost nothing about it. They have settled for the "pursuit of happiness," which

Joy comes as a by-product.

has come to mean the acquisition of people, possessions, and favorable circumstances. And since whatever affects the world also affects the church, Christians in America are stunted in their capacity for joy.

Joy is not so easily obtained, however, as momentary happiness might be. Joy is deeper. Joy is not dependent on favorable circumstances, but on a proper outlook on life.

You may be euphoric if you win $10 million in a publisher's sweepstakes. You may be ecstatic if you receive a job promotion. You may be thrilled when you drive your new car off the lot. But none of these things will give you lasting joy—only momentary happiness.

Joy does not come by pursuing joy. Joy comes as a by-product of pursuing God and the good of others. Since American society elevates self above others, it knows very little about true joy.

I have been captain of a victorious athletic team, out in the middle of a basketball floor, receiving a trophy for winning a tournament, with hundreds of screaming fans voicing their delirious approval. That was one of the happiest experiences of my life, but there was no joy. Joy is knowing that God will somehow get me through whatever trial I face, and that in the end, all will be well.

I also have been at the bedside of someone dying of Lou Gehrig's disease. She had lost control of bodily movement and was quickly losing the ability to talk or swallow. In just a few days, she would have to be fed artificially and eventually put on a respirator. We both knew she would die a terrible death quite soon. We talked about Jesus, and death, and heaven. It was one of the unhappiest moments of my life, but there was deep joy.

Happiness and joy don't always go together.

If we live for the same things the world lives for (people, possessions, and favorable circumstances), then instead of experiencing joy, we will experience constant frustration. We will be frustrated over not being able to control things completely enough or long enough for our life to be consistently "happy" and frustrated with God for not blessing our lives and answering our selfish prayers. Furthermore, if we were able to get enough control (or enough luck) to get life going our way consistently, life would soon become meaningless. We were not created to live for ourselves; we were created to live for God and for others. We will never know joy any other way.

What Is Peace?

Peace is the absence of anxiety and the presence of trusting assurance in the promises of God.

The third fruit of the Spirit, peace, is a gift that the Holy Spirit gives us when we believe the promises of God. Most Christians would say that they believe the promises of God. When we feel turmoil in our lives, however, it is often because of a promise in Scripture that we do not know about, do not understand, or do not believe. In Matthew 6:19–34 we are promised that God will feed and clothe us. Then it exhorts us to "not worry about tomorrow, for tomorrow will worry about its own things. Sufficient for the day is its own trouble" (v. 34). Yet I do find myself agitated and in turmoil over tomorrow. I fear that God will not be true to His word. When I see a problem that appears to have no solution, I often get anxious rather than resting in the fact that God knows the solution.

The Lord ministered to me deeply during one difficult time in my life as I read the account of the parting of the Red Sea in Exodus 14. The Israelites had left Egypt and were camped on the west bank of the Red Sea. The sea was to the east of them, mountains to the north and south, and then, here came the Egyptian army bearing down on them from the west. On three sides they were hemmed in, and now catastrophe was pressing down on them on the fourth side, with no solution in sight. God told Moses to stand still and see the salvation of the Lord. Then God parted the Red Sea, allowing the Israelites an escape route.

God has solutions we cannot see.

Often in our lives there is no solution to our problems on the horizon, but God lives beyond the horizon and can bring solutions we cannot foresee. We must remember that God has promised to see us through the trials of this life. If we trust His promises, we can have peace in the midst of difficult circumstances. God has assured us that in this life all things work together for good to those who love Him, and that no temptation will overtake us but that He will provide a way of escape that we might be able to bear it. The Scriptures are laden with promises that, as we have the grace to believe, will build peace into the core of our being.

This does not mean that life will always be easy. On the contrary, life is often filled with physical pain, emotional turmoil, spiritual upheaval. So we must understand peace not as an elimination of troubling circumstances, but as an assurance and trust in God in spite of our circumstances. In the midst of fighting the trials of life you might sometimes hear me say, "I am okay at the core. I'm just a little frayed around the edges." Life certainly will "fray" us around the edges, but at the core, as we grow in the grace and knowledge of our Lord Jesus Christ, the fruit of the Spirit increasingly can be ours.

Conclusion

The fruit of the Spirit is just that. It is not the fruit merely of self-effort, though some self-effort is required of the Christian before he will experience the fruit. But self-effort alone will not produce the fruit of the Spirit.

Remember the experience I described earlier of when as a young Christian I became exceedingly frustrated at the lack of progress in my spiritual life? I had doubled my efforts in prayer, Scripture study, memorization, and reading, as well as my witnessing and service to God; but my intensified efforts produced nothing. I felt that God wanted me to be more spiritual than I was, but no matter how hard I tried, I could not seem to speed up my growth.

The breakthrough began for me when I heard a seminary professor say, "You can't be holy in a hurry." No one had ever told me before that God was willing to put up with my immaturities, much as a parent is willing to put up with a two-year-old's immaturities. The parent certainly looks forward to the day when the two-year-old will grow out of the "terrible twos," but until that time the parent will not expect more than reasonable progress.

God does not ask more than we can give.

As I look back at that experience more than twenty-five years later, I see I was, like any child, impatient to be more mature. However, my desire was frustrated by the assumption that God expected me to be more mature than I was. When I understood that God was not asking more of me than I could give, I was able to be satisfied and dissatisfied with my spiritual life at the same time. I was dissatisfied in that I wanted to be more mature and knew that God eventually expected me to be more mature. But I could be satisfied in the sense that, if the fruit of the Spirit did not come purely by my own effort, and if my present stage of spiritual growth was all the Holy Spirit had given me, I had to be content with the work of God in my life. It is always God's perfect will that we be like Jesus, but it is within His permissive will that He gives us time to grow into His likeness.

Speed Bump!

Slow down to be sure you've gotten the main points of this chapter.

Question
Answer

Q1. What is the fruit of the Spirit?

A1. The fruit of the Spirit are character qualities that God possesses and that the Holy Spirit *imparts* to us as we live in trusting obedience to Jesus.

Q2. What is love?

A2. Love is the steady direction of our *will* toward the lasting good of another.

Q3. What is joy?

A3. Joy is a deep sense of *well-being* that is not dependent upon favorable circumstances, but rooted in a fundamental acceptance of, and confidence in, the will of God.

Q4. What is peace?

A4. Peace is the absence of anxiety and the presence of trusting assurance in the *promises* of God.

Fill in the Blank

Question
Answer

Q1. What is the fruit of the Spirit?

A1. The fruit of the Spirit are character qualities that God possesses and that the Holy Spirit _____ to us as we live in trusting obedience to Jesus.

Q2. What is love?

A2. Love is the steady direction of our _____ toward the lasting good of another.

Q3. What is joy?

A3. Joy is a deep sense of _____ that is not dependent upon favorable circumstances, but rooted in a fundamental acceptance of, and confidence in, the will of God.

Q4.   What is peace?

A4.   Peace is the absence of anxiety and the presence of trusting assurance
in the _____ of God.

For Further Thought and Discussion

1.   How do you assess your own spiritual growth? Have you grown as
rapidly as you thought you should or would?

2.   To what degree do you think your spiritual growth has been hampered
by your own lack of effort, and how much do you think is simply the
fact that it takes time to grow spiritually?

3.   On a scale of 1 to 10 (1 = nonexistent, 10 = total Christlikeness), how
would you rate the fruit of love, joy, and peace in your life?

4.   What do you think you could do to experience a fuller measure of these
characteristics?

What If I Don't Believe?

1.   If I don't believe that the Spirit produces these fruit in my life, I might
get confused trying to generate them myself.

2.   Or, I might become defeated when my self-efforts are not effective.

3.   If I do not believe that these are qualities that God has, and wants me to
have, I might be content to go through life without these qualities in my
life. Or, I might be distressed with life in general because I do not
possess these characteristics, but not understand why I am distressed.

For Further Study

1. Scripture
Several passages speak of the fruit of the Spirit, and of love, joy, and peace.
Study them further to see how they add to your understanding of these issues.

*   John 14:1–3, 27

*   John 15:1–11

- 1 Corinthians 13:4–7

- Galatians 5:22–23

2. Books

Books that deal with the fruit of the Spirit are not very plentiful. The most helpful one I have found is listed below.

The Holy Spirit, Billy Graham

Lord, teach me to silence my own heart that I may listen to the gentle movement of the Holy Spirit within me and sense the depths which are of God.
■ **Elijah de Vidas (Sixteenth Century)**

12

What Is the Fruit of the Spirit? (Part Two)

The story is told of a man in South Africa many years ago when diamonds were just being discovered there. Like gold fever, or any other addiction, this man became consumed with the possibility of becoming fabulously wealthy. He sold his farm in South Africa and used the money to begin a search for what he hoped would be incalculable wealth.

Reality was much more difficult than the dream, however, and the man exhausted his health and his wealth, but still was no closer to his fortune in diamonds than he was the day he sold the farm. Finally, penniless and broken physically and mentally, he threw himself into a river and drowned.

Meanwhile, the young man who had bought the farm was tending to his work one day when he found an unusual-looking stone in a creek bed. There were many similar stones, but this one was the largest and most distinctive. He put it on his fireplace mantle as an object of interest.

One day a visitor in the young farmer's home saw the stone. He picked it up, turning it over and over, scrutinizing it intently. He then turned to the farmer and announced that this might very well be a diamond, and if so, one of the largest ever discovered. Under a cloud of utmost secrecy, the stone was analyzed and confirmed to be one of the largest and finest diamonds ever found.

Still operating with great secrecy, the farmer searched the stream, gathering all similar stones, and all of them were diamonds too. The farm was covered with diamonds, lying in streams and on the surface of the ground, just waiting to be picked up. In fact, this farm that was sold by the first adventurer so that he could roam the country in search of fabulous wealth turned out to be one of the richest diamond deposits in the world.

And so it is with life. We often go in search of life's treasures when we already possess them. It is merely a variation of the parable that the "bluebird of happiness" is in our own backyard.

In this chapter we learn that . . .

1. Patience is the ability to endure unpleasant people or circumstances for a higher cause.
2. Kindness is treating others well in word and deed.
3. Goodness is doing that which is beneficial for others.
4. Faithfulness is being reliable in doing what you should do.
5. Gentleness is treating others carefully, with respect and sensitivity.
6. Self-control is the ability to resist immediate gratification for the sake of a higher goal.

This principle especially applies to the issue of the Christian life. Christians often get duped into searching for happiness, meaning, purpose, and joy in the same places the world looks for them: people, possessions, and favorable circumstances. In doing so, they exhaust themselves and end up dissatisfied, disillusioned, and even broken.

What they long for they already possess. The Holy Spirit lives within them, and He is willing to pour out in their lives His fruit—love, joy, and peace. If we had those three qualities in our lives, what more could we ask for? Yet, in Galatians 5:22–23, the apostle Paul goes on to mention six other fruit of the Spirit that, if possessed, are not only deeply satisfying to the one possessing them, but also help us to have rich relationships with other people and make us good "living advertisements" for Christianity to unbelievers. The wealth we long for is spiritual wealth, ours to be had if we live in obedience to the Holy Spirit.

In the previous chapter, we looked at the first three of the fruit of the Spirit: love, joy, and peace. In this chapter, we want to look at the remaining six.

What Is Patience?

Patience is the ability to endure unpleasant people or circumstances for a higher cause.

I heard of a man who decided to get away from the rat race of the corporate world, so he joined a monastery that required a vow of silence. Just the thing, he thought, for reducing the frustration and upheaval of his former life. In the monastery, he was allowed to say two words every five years.

After the first five years, he was called into his superior's office, who asked, "Do you have anything you would like to say? You have two words."

The man said, "Bad food!"

He returned to his life at the monastery, and after another five years he was again given the opportunity to say two words.

"Hard bed!" he said, and returned once more to his normal life at the monastery.

Five years passed again, and again he was before his superior, who asked him if he had two words he would like to say.

The man said, "I quit!"

His superior said, "Well, I'm not surprised. You've done nothing but complain since you got here!"

Patience is relative, I suppose. His "superior" thought he had done nothing but complain since he arrived, but I thought he exercised some pretty amazing patience. He endured bad food and a hard bed for fifteen years with only four words of complaint. I thought he seemed like a pretty patient person.

Patience (or long-suffering in the King James Version), the fruit of the Spirit, comes from a Greek word that means to re-

---

Why I need to know this

1. I need to know this so that I will have a complete view of the maturity level that God wants me to have.
2. I need to know this so that I will not excuse weaknesses in my character.
3. I need to know this so that I will trust God to make me mature and not think that I can do it on my own.

---

main steadfast under provocation. It means "hanging in there" when you feel like you are merely hanging. It carries the thought of patiently enduring bad treatment without retaliation or revenge. If we are irritable, vengeful, resentful, or malicious in our relationships with others, we are "short-suffering," not "long-suffering."

It is a difficult virtue to get and keep, as you well know if you have ever been treated unjustly or accused of something falsely by someone you thought was your friend. Patience can prove elusive if you have been passed up for a promotion, or failed to get a job, with the position going to someone whom you believed to be your inferior. A spouse who treats you badly or ignores you requires enormous patience, as does someone who tells a hurtful truth about you in an unkind way.

We also need patience in the face of other problems: illness or injury that takes a long time to heal, or never heals; financial problems you are powerless to overcome; loved ones who are self-destructing through drugs, alcohol, sex, or crime; or under-achievement in your vocation or home.

Patience is a virtue that the Holy Spirit will build into our lives as we live in trusting obedience to Him. The apostle Paul wrote that we can be "strengthened with all might, according to His glorious power, for all patience and longsuffering with joy" (Colossians 1:11). Patience comes from the power of God when we rely on Him, refusing to give in to our natural inclinations to lash out or withdraw—to give in to anger or despair. Even when the current of events is flowing against us, we must swim up the emotional stream of life and allow the Holy Spirit to empower us with patience.

What Is Kindness?

Kindness is treating others well in word and deed.

Abraham Joshua Heschel, a Jewish rabbi, used to say, "When I was young, I admired clever people. Now that I am old, I admire kind people." (Harold Kushner, *When All You've Ever Wanted Isn't Enough*, p. 58). I'm with Rabbi Heschel. The older I get, the more I admire kind people. Kindness is one of the greatest virtues and most admired, even while it is one of the rarest. How many acts of kindness have you witnessed lately? How many acts of kindness have you *done* lately? We admire kindness when we see it, and we appreciate it when we experience it, but we often shy away from acts of kindness ourselves. Kindness often costs us something, and we fear becoming a victim, unsure whether we are actually performing an act of kindness or getting taken in by someone.

I remember several years ago seeing a woman standing be-side a busy street in the cold with a sign in her hand, "Need money to get home. Willing to work." I drove past her, as did thousands of other people, and just as I had with many other people before. But this time it was different. The Holy Spirit got a headlock on me and wouldn't let me go. I couldn't forget that young woman. It was Thanksgiving weekend and very cold out. Her nose was running, her eyes were red, her hands were chapped. I thought, "If this lady is trying to find an 'easy way out' in life, she miscalculated. What she is doing is harder than working."

I talked to her, and she said she was trying to get home and ran out of money. She couldn't get a job, because all the likely places to get a job (fast-food restaurants, etc.) required that she have a phone number, and she didn't have one. She was staying at a rescue mission, so she wasn't starving to death, but she was between a rock and a hard place. To this day, I don't know if her problem was legitimate or not, but I gave her enough money for a bus ticket home, which was not an insignificant amount of money. She might have bought cocaine with the money for all I know. However, the issue right then was not between her and me. It was between God and me. He wanted to know if I cared enough about people to risk getting taken in.

I am not suggesting that everyone ought to give money to people like that. All I know is that God used that moment to test me. Who owned the money in my bank account? Who prioritized the time it took me to talk to her and then go to the bank and get the money? I performed an act of kindness that day, but I almost shied away because I wasn't sure I wanted to pay the price.

> **God wants to know if we care enough to pay the price.**

A thousand other opportunities for acts of kindness can be missed for the same reason, but on a smaller scale. My wife and I used to live in a neighborhood in which a lot of minority students would come by selling candy and "nicknacks" we didn't need. Initially I responded by just nicely getting rid of them. But I didn't feel good about it. They were, I became persuaded, doing the best thing they knew to earn a little money. I had sold door-to-door before and knew it wasn't easy. I began to admire their "grit." So I changed my strategy. Instead of getting rid of them, I began asking the kids how much profit they made on their monster candy bar. Then, instead of buying the candy bar, I would give them the amount of profit they would have made if I had bought the candy (I didn't want to eat the thing). If they were selling worthless things, I would often buy them anyway, just to be kind and encourage them in their enterprise. Proverbs 19:17 says, "He who is gracious to a poor man lends to the LORD, and He will repay him for his good deed" (NASB).

By giving these examples, I am not suggesting that everyone follow my example. I am not even saying that I would do the same thing again in every instance. I am just saying that we must be alert to opportunities to be kind to others and respond when the Lord prompts us.

We also can be kind to those in spiritual or emotional need. I once read, "We should always be kind to others, for they may be walking life's road wounded." How that struck me. I had walked wounded many times, and I was profoundly grateful when others were kind to me.

Be alert for those who are walking life's road wounded.

I will never forget something that happened when I was in seminary. Those were difficult times. Seminary was extremely demanding academically. I had to work so much that I didn't have enough time to study, but I had to study so much that I couldn't work enough to make a decent living (I just heard a loud amen from fellow seminarians). Time and money were too short for many friends or recreation. I was pretty discouraged.

One morning I pulled into the seminary parking lot for my first class, and the professor pulled in at the same time. He got out of his car, turned to wait for me, greeted me, and chatted amiably as he walked me into the classroom. As long as I live I will never forget that simple act of kindness. He was not even conscious of having done anything, but it fed me deeply, spiritually and emotionally. Memory of that simple incident has spurred me to be alert for opportunities to be kind.

I try especially to be kind to people at checkout counters and other such places where people often aren't kind to them. I try to have a pleasant word to say. I believe that if we cultivate the habit of kindness in small things, we will also be even more ready to be kind in bigger things.

I fail many times when I am preoccupied or hurting a little myself. We all do. But be kind to others. You may be lending to the Lord, and the person you are kind to may be walking life's road wounded. Think how grateful you would be in their shoes. Use discretion, but be sensitive. Be ready to be kind whenever you think Jesus would be kind.

What Is Goodness?
Goodness is doing that which is beneficial for others.

Goodness and kindness are so similar that it is often hard to distinguish between the two. I don't know if it is a valid distinction, but I often think of kindness as being very personal, face to face, whereas goodness need not always be as personal. Someone might give a sum of money to help build a hospital. That gesture, to me, seems more good than kind, because it is an indirect benefit to people rather than a direct benefit. The benefactor might not even give the money to an individual but to a nonprofit corporation. People you don't even know and never see, months and years later, reap the benefits.

I read a story, recently, of ricocheting goodness:

V. P. Menon was a significant political figure in India during its struggle for independence from Britain after World War II. He was the highest-ranking Indian in the government, and it was to him that Lord Mountbatten turned for the final drafting of the charter plan for independence.

Eldest son of twelve children, he quit school at thirteen and worked as a laborer, coal miner, factory hand, merchant, and schoolteacher. He talked his way into a job as a clerk in the Indian administration, and his rise was meteoric—largely because of his integrity and brilliant skills in working with both Indian and British officials in a productive way. Both Nehru and Mountbatten mentioned his name with highest praise as one who made practical freedom possible for his country.

He had a reputation for personal charity which began when Menon arrived in Delhi to seek a job in government, and all his possessions, including his money and I.D., were stolen at the railroad station. In desperation he turned to an elderly Sikh, explained his troubles, and asked for a temporary loan of fifteen rupees to tide him over until he could get a job. The Sikh gave him the money. When Menon asked for his address so that he could repay the man, the Sikh said that Menon owed the debt to any stranger who came to him in need, as long as he lived. The help came from a stranger and was to be repaid to a stranger.

Menon never forgot that debt—neither the gift of trust nor the fifteen rupees. He was generous to the needy the rest of his life.

This story was told to me by a man whose name I do not know. He was standing beside me in the Bombay airport at the left-baggage counter. I had come to reclaim my bags and had no Indian currency left. The agent would not take a traveler's check, and I was uncertain about getting my luggage and making my plane. The man paid my claim-check fee—about eighty cents—and told me the story as a way of refusing my attempt to figure out how to repay him. His father had been Menon's assistant and had learned Menon's charitable ways and passed them on to his son. The son had continued the tradition of seeing himself in debt to strangers, whenever, however. (Excerpted from Robert Fulghum, *All I Really Need to Know I Learned in Kindergarten* 154-155.)

That's good—very good. We all ought to try to do more good than we do. Everyone wins.

What Is Faithfulness?

Faithfulness is being reliable in doing what you should do.

Clarence Jordan was a man of unusual abilities and commitment. He had two Ph.D.s, one in agriculture and one in Greek and Hebrew. He could have chosen to do anything he wanted. He chose to serve the poor. In the 1940s, he founded Koinonia Farm in Americus, Georgia. It was a community for poor whites and poor blacks—an idea that did not go over well in the Deep South of the '40s.

Ironically, much of the resistance came from good church people who were as committed to the laws of segregation as the other folk in town. For fourteen years the town people tried everything to stop Clarence. They tried boycotting him, and slashing workers' tires when they came to town, with no effect.

Finally, in 1954, the Ku Klux Klan had enough of Clarence Jordan, so they decided to get rid of him once and for all. They came one night with guns and torches and set fire to every building on Koinonia Farm but Clarence's home, which they riddled with bullets. And they chased off all the families except one black family which refused to leave.

Clarence recognized the voices of many of the Klansmen, and some of them were church people. Another was the local newspaper's reporter. The next day, the reporter came out to see what remained of the farm. The rubble still smoldered and the land was scorched, but he found Clarence in the field, hoeing and planting.

"I heard the awful news," he called to Clarence, "and I came out to do a story on the tragedy of your farm closing."

Clarence just kept on hoeing and planting. The reporter kept prodding, trying to get a rise from this quietly determined man who seemed to be planting instead of packing his bags. Finally, the reporter said in a haughty voice, "Well, Dr. Jordan, you got two of them Ph.D.s and you've put fourteen years into this farm, and there's nothing left of it at all. Just how successful do you think you've been?"

Clarence stopped hoeing, turned toward the reporter with his penetrating blue eyes, and said quietly but firmly, "About as successful as the cross. Sir, I don't think you understand us. What we are about is not success but faithfulness. We're staying. Good day." Beginning that day, Clarence and his companions rebuilt Koinonia and the farm is going strong today. (Excerpted from Tim Hansel, *Holy Sweat* 188-189.)

Faithfulness is being trustworthy; it is "hanging in there"; it is persevering. It is being the kind of person who can be counted on to do what is right. Over and over in the Bible, we are admonished to be faithful. Matthew 25:21 says that if we are faithful in little things, the Lord will give us bigger things. In Revelation 2:10 we read, "Be faithful until death, and I will give you the crown of life."

We should be faithful to our word. We should be faithful to our responsibilities. But above all we should be faithful to God. God wants to be able to count on us. If we let Him, the Holy Spirit will help make us faithful people. Do you have a weakness in being faithful? Many do. It is not a highly valued characteristic in modern America. But it is highly valued to God.

What Is Gentleness?

Gentleness is treating others carefully, with respect and sensitivity.

A parable is told about the sun and the wind arguing which one was more powerful. The sun quietly asserted that he was the strongest, while the wind protested loudly.

"See that traveler walking along the road down there?" the

wind asked. "Whichever of us makes him take his coat off first is the most powerful." The sun agreed.

The wind blew short, violent bursts to rip the coat off the traveler, but the man only clutched the coat closer to himself. The wind escalated to great, furious gales, but to no avail. The traveler simply wrapped his coat about him as tightly as possible and leaned into the punishing wind.

Finally, the wind was exhausted and could blow no longer. Then the sun came out and began shining soft, gentle light upon the traveler. After a while, a little bead of perspiration began to roll down the traveler's forehead. Before long, the coat came off, as the traveler succumbed to the sun's gentle warmth.

In human relationships, gentleness is like the sun, and aggression is like the wind. One disarms while the other antagonizes.

Gentleness is being easy on others, taking into account their vulnerable points, and taking care not to hurt them. I recently had

Goodness is love under discipline.

some dental work done in a clinic where more than one dentist worked on me. One dentist had rough hands; the other had gentle hands. The first dentist hurt me; the second one didn't. That is part of what it means to be gentle.

The biblical word translated "gentle" goes beyond this limited meaning of the word. It is sometimes translated "meek." One who is meek is often understood to be timid, weak, and "wimpy." Such is not the case, however. The Greek word carries with it the idea of "power under control." Until he was matured by the Holy Spirit, the apostle Peter was loud and pushy. Then, he became controlled and channeled, using his great energy for the glory of God. Moses is mentioned in the Bible as the "meekest" man who ever lived. Yet he was far from a wimp. He was a dramatic and powerful leader, but under the control of God. A river that is controlled can generate much power. A fire under control can warm a house. A personality under control can be used by God for His purposes. Controlled energy can achieve great good. Uncontrolled energy usually just destroys.

Jesus was arrested, taken through a series of mock trials, beaten, and mistreated. He had the power to annihilate his tormentors with a spoken word, but He didn't, choosing instead to endure suffering for the sake of our redemption. Isaiah spoke prophetically when he said of Jesus, "He was oppressed and He was afflicted, yet He opened not His mouth; He was led as a lamb to the slaughter, and as a sheep before its shearers is silent, so He opened not His mouth" (Isaiah 53:7). Meekness is "love under control."

The Holy Spirit will build gentleness within us. When He does, we do not hurt people or run roughshod over them. We do not "lock horns" with those who cross us. Rather, under the control of the Holy Spirit, we display sensitivity to others and allow God to channel our energy for the good of others.

What Is Self-control?

Self-control is the ability to resist immediate gratification for the sake of a higher goal.

Someone once said, "I can resist everything except temptation." That's the way it is with most of us. I have found that I can do whatever I want to do—except make myself want to do the right thing *all* the time. The Holy Spirit, however, cannot be tempted, and He does want to do the right thing all the time. So, what we lack in self-control, the Holy Spirit can supply.

A person without self-control is like a ship at full sail in a strong wind with no rudder. People without self-discipline miss deadlines, are always late, eat too much, get too angry too often, drink too much, become too sexually involved, are too lazy, watch too much TV, speak too often without concern for others, **Living without control can waste your life.** fail to perform up to their potential, act dishonestly, etc., etc., etc. Lack of self-control is a life-wasting, life-destroying thing.

By nature and natural habit I am not a self-disciplined person. Yet I discovered in my college years that I would never get the things I wanted in life unless I paid the price. That required self-discipline. There are people who say to me now, "I am amazed at how disciplined you are." To that, I can only respond, "That is the Holy Spirit." He is the one who gave me the insight and conviction that I needed self-discipline, and then He built His discipline in me.

Self-control is one of the most difficult character qualities to possess, because we don't want to do the things we should. If we wanted to do them, it wouldn't take self-control. Yet, it is also one of the greatest character qualities to possess. Solomon said, "He who is slow to anger is better than the mighty, and he who rules his spirit than he who takes a city" (Proverbs 16:32).

What is your area of greatest weakness? The Holy Spirit wants to give you self-control in this area. However, we often have to mature or grow into self-control, which obviously takes time. In the meantime, we can help protect ourselves by getting others to help us. It might be our pastor, or members of a Bible study or other small group, or someone who will agree to disciple us. We in America are so independent that we think we can and should do everything alone. But God did not intend for Christians to strive alone. He intended us to be so involved in one another's lives that we would strengthen one another and help one another do the things we ought to do and not do the things we ought not to do. And, of course, we can pray for one another that the Holy Spirit will give us the self-control we need to live lives that honor Him.

Conclusion

In conclusion, I want to make four observations.

1. I doubt if the list of the fruit of the Spirit is exhaustive. The apostle Paul listed the works of the flesh in Galatians 5:19–21. Certainly, his list of sins was not exhaustive. Now, in the next two verses, he lists the fruit of the Spirit; and they, too, are probably not exhaustive. But they are representative. These kinds of character qualities are true of the Holy Spirit, and He wants them to be true of us. In time, He will give us even more.

2. The fruit of the Spirit are a unit. Paul calls them the *fruit* of the Spirit, not the *fruits* of the Spirit. That is, they are a "whole" and when you get one of the list, you are on

The fruit of the Spirit are related to spiritual maturity.

your way to them all. For example, a person would not be "loving" if he were not also "kind." He would not be "good" if he were not also "gentle." I like the idea that these are not nine "fruits" but nine facets of one fruit.

Certainly, because of temperament, upbringing, culture, and background, some of the fruit may come more easily to a person than others. For example, one might find kindness coming more quickly then self-control. However, the Holy Spirit brings spiritual maturity, and maturity covers all nine characteristics.

3. These are the fruit of the Spirit, not the fruit of self-effort. We are to strive for obedience to Christ. We are not to be passive in the pursuit of Christ's character. Yet even in our best pursuit, we must be patient and wait for the Spirit to build these qualities into our lives as a whole fruit.

4. Just because love, joy, peace, etc. are fruit of the Spirit does not mean non-Christians cannot experience them, at least in some measure. Many non-Christians are kind and self-controlled. It isn't that all people who manifest these character qualities are mature Christians, but that all mature Christians will manifest these character qualities.

The bottom line is that these character qualities reflect the spirit and nature of God. As we mature and allow the Holy Spirit to rule our lives, God is glorified, our lives are enriched and satisfied, and the unsaved are given a favorable picture of God by what they see of Him in our lives.

Speed Bump!

Slow down to make sure you've gotten the main points of this chapter.

Question & Answer

Q1. What is patience?

A1. Patience is the ability to *endure* unpleasant people or circumstances for a higher cause.

Q2. What is kindness?

A2. Kindness is treating others *well* in word and deed.

Q3. What is goodness?

A3. Goodness is doing that which is *beneficial* for others.

Q4. What is faithfulness?

A4. Faithfulness is being *reliable* in doing what you should do.

Q5. What is gentleness?

A5. Gentleness is treating others *carefully,* with respect and sensitivity.

Q6. What is self-control?

A6. Self-control is the ability to *resist* immediate gratification for the sake of a higher goal.

Fill in the Blank

Question   **Q1.** What is patience?

Answer   **A1.** Patience is the ability to _____ unpleasant people or circumstances for a higher cause.

Q2. What is kindness?

A2. Kindness is treating others _____ in word and deed.

Q3. What is goodness?

A3. Goodness is doing that which is _____ for others.

Q4. What is faithfulness?

A4. Faithfulness is being _____ in doing what you should do.

Q5. What is gentleness?

A5. Gentleness is treating others _____, with respect and sensitivity.

Q6. What is self-control?

A6. Self-control is the ability to _____ immediate gratification for the sake of a higher goal.

For Further Thought and Discussion

1. Have you ever thought that you have possessed one of the fruit of the Spirit only to lose it again? How do you explain that?

2. Which fruit come more easily to you than others? Which ones come less easily? Why do you think so? What do you think you can do to cooperate with God's plan in your life to "even them out"?

3. What person do you admire for his/her character? Describe what you admire about the person and why you admire it.

What If I Don't Believe?

1. If I don't believe that the fruit of the Spirit is a unit of nine, I might miss out on a character quality God wants me to have.

2. If I don't believe that the fruit are a unit, I might excuse a weakness in one area when I shouldn't. I may deceive myself into thinking that I am spiritually mature when I am not.

3. If I don't believe the fruit of the Spirit is God-generated, I may become impatient or defeated at my slow pace of growth.

For Further Study

1. Scripture
Several passages speak of the fruit of the Spirit, and of love, joy, and peace. Study them further to see how they add to your understanding of these issues.

- John 14:1–3, 27

- John 15:1–11

- 1 Corinthians 13:4–7

- Galatians 5:22–23

2. Books
Not many books deal at length with the fruit of the Spirit. The most helpful one I have found is listed below.

The Holy Spirit, Billy Graham

Bibliography

Anders, Max E. *30 Days to Understanding the Bible*. Dallas: Word, Inc., 1992.

Anders, Max E. *30 Days to Understanding How to Live as a Christian*. Dallas: Word, Inc., 1994.

Black, Carl. "All in a Day's Work," *Reader's Digest*. August 1993.

Brand, Paul, and Philip Yancey. *Fearfully and Wonderfully Made*. Grand Rapids: Zondervan, 1980.

Elwell, Walter (ed.). *Evangelical Dictionary of Theology*. Grand Rapids: Baker Book House Co., 1984.

Foss, Sam Walter. "The House by the Side of the Road." Quoted by William Bennett in *The Book of Virtues*. New York: Simon & Schuster, 1993.

Fulghum, Robert. *All I Really Need to Know I Learned in Kindergarten*. New York: Villard Books, 1988.

Graham, Billy. *The Holy Spirit*. Dallas: Word, Inc., 1988.

Green, Michael P. *Illustrations for Biblical Preaching*. Grand Rapids: Baker Book House Co., 1988.

Haggai, John. *Winning over Pain, Fear and Worry*. New York: Inspirational Press, 1991.

Hansel, Tim. *Holy Sweat*. Dallas: Word, Inc., 1987.

Kushner, Harold. *When All You've Ever Wanted Isn't Enough*. Thorndike, ME: Large Print Books, 1987.

Lewis, C. S. *The Four Loves*. San Diego, CA: Harvest Books, 1991.

Neill, Stephen. *The Christian Character*. New York: Association Press, 1955.

Packer, James I. *Concise Theology*. Wheaton, IL: Tyndale, 1993.

Packer, James I. *Keep in Step with the Holy Spirit*. Grand Rapids: Fleming H. Revell, 1987.

Schaeffer, Francis. "The Mark of a Christian." Appendix to *The Church at the End of the 20th Century*. Downer's Grove, IL: InterVarsity Press, 1970.

Schaeffer, Francis. *True Spirituality*. Wheaton, IL: Tyndale, 1972.

ten Boom, Corrie. *Tramp for the Lord*. Fort Washington, PA: Christian Literature Crusade, Inc., 1974.

Vine, W. E. *Vine's Expository Dictionary of New Testament Words*. Nashville: Royal Publishers, Inc., 1939.

Wallace, Lew. *Ben Hur*. Provo, UT: Regal Publications, 1993.

Yancey, Philip. "Vital Issues." *Guidance*. Portland, OR: Multnomah Press, 1983.

Master Review

Chapter 1

Question
Answer

Q1. Why believe the Holy Spirit is a person?

A1. The Scriptures reveal the Holy Spirit to be a person, with all the living characteristics of a *personal* being.

Q2. Why believe the Holy Spirit is God?

A2. The Scriptures reveal the Holy Spirit to be God, with all the defining characteristics of a *divine* being.

Q3. Why believe the Holy Spirit is a member of the Trinity?

A3. The Scriptures reveal the Holy Spirit to be on an *equal* level with the Father and the Son though distinct from them in role.

Chapter 2

Q1. What did the Holy Spirit do in the Old Testament?

A1. In the Old Testament, the Holy Spirit *helped* in creation, revealed truth to people, and empowered people to do God's will.

Q2. What did the Holy Spirit do in the New Testament?

A2. In the New Testament, the Holy Spirit empowered the ministry of Jesus and His church.

Q3. What does the Holy Spirit do today?

A3. Today, the Holy Spirit *helps* Christians know, be, and do what God wants.

Q4. What will the Holy Spirit do in the future?

A4. In the future, the Holy Spirit will *help* bring history to an end and usher in eternity.

Chapter 3

Q1. What is conviction?

A1. Conviction is the ministry of the Holy Spirit in which He causes us to recognize our *sin* and prompts us to turn from it.

Q2. What is regeneration?

A2. Regeneration is the ministry of the Holy Spirit in which He causes us to be *born again*, spiritually, resulting in eternal life.

Q3. What is indwelling?

A3. Indwelling is the ministry of the Holy Spirit coming to *live* in the body of each Christian.

Q4. What is baptism?

A4. Baptism of the Holy Spirit is the ministry of the Spirit *incorporating* the Christian into the body of Christ.

Q5. What is sealing?

A5. Sealing of the Holy Spirit is the ministry of the Spirit *marking* us as God's own possession and guaranteeing our salvation.

Chapter 4

Q1. How does the Holy Spirit make the Christian feel secure?

A1. The Holy Spirit gives a Christian inner *assurance* of salvation.

Q2. How does the Holy Spirit teach the Christian?

A2. The Holy Spirit divinely enables a Christian to *understand* Scripture in a way that he could not before becoming a Christian.

Q3. How does the Holy Spirit lead and guide us?

A3. The Holy Spirit leads and guides Christians by putting it in our hearts and minds to do His *will* and by providentially governing our circumstances.

Q4. How does the Holy Spirit help us pray?

A4. The Holy Spirit encourages and enables us to pray, and even prays to God the Father *for* us when we don't know what to pray.

Chapter 5

Q1. What is the goal of spiritual change?

A1. The goal of spiritual change is *transformation* into the spiritual likeness of Jesus.

Q2. What is at the heart of spiritual change?

A2. At the heart of spiritual change is an *interaction* in which the Holy Spirit prompts and the individual responds.

Q3. What process must we go through to become like Christ?

A3. To become like Christ requires the *combination* of the work of God, the word of God, personal commitment, other believers, and time and trials.

Q4. Why don't we change more quickly and more completely?

A4. We don't change more quickly and more completely because God has decreed that we be transformed over *time* and because of the complications of sin.

Chapter 6

Q1. What is a spiritual gift?

A1. A spiritual gift is a God-given *ability* for ministry to others.

Q2. What are the office gifts?

A2. Office gifts are given to those who serve the church at large in a *specific* capacity: apostle, prophet, evangelist, and pastor-teacher.

Q3. What are the service gifts?

A3. Service gifts are *nonmiraculous* gifts that correspond to ministries that all of us should do, but some individuals are gifted for greater impact in these ministries.

Q4. What are special gifts?

A4. Special gifts are *miraculous* or supernormal gifts that appear to be given for the purpose not only of meeting a need of the moment but also for validating the message of Christianity to those who have not heard or believed.

Chapter 7

Q1. What is the Durative position?

A1. The Durative position is the belief that the signs and wonders in the New Testament have continued throughout church history and still exist *today*.

Q2. What is the Cessationist position?

A2. The Cessationist position states that New Testament signs and wonders *disappeared* with the passing of the apostles and the establishment of the Scriptures and are not intended ever to reappear again.

Q3. What is the Approximation position?

A3. The Approximation position holds that the miraculous gifts and signs and wonders are not fully operative today, but that a *reduced* form of the gifts operates today under the apparent blessing of God.

Chapter 8

Q1. What is the Pentecostal/charismatic interpretation of Ephesians 5:18?

A1. The Pentecostal/charismatic interpretation is that the filling of the Spirit here neither requires nor rules out super-normal *experiences* such as speaking in tongues.

Q2. What is the "victorious Christian life" interpretation of Ephesians 5:18?

A2. The "victorious Christian life" interpretation is that the filling of the Spirit *empowers* a person for improved Christian living and greater ministry.

Q3. What is the "word of Christ" interpretation of Ephesians 5:18?

A3. The "word of Christ" interpretation is that the filling of the Spirit is essentially the same as "letting the *word* of Christ dwell in you richly."

Chapter 9

Q1. Can we sin so often that God will not forgive us?

A1. We *cannot* sin so *often* that God will not forgive us.

Q2. Can we sin so badly that God will not forgive us?

A2. We *cannot* sin so *badly* that God will not forgive us.

Q3. What is the unpardonable sin?

A3. The unpardonable sin is *rejecting* the Holy Spirit's pull to bring us to Christ.

Chapter 10

Q1. What does it mean to grieve the Holy Spirit?

A1. We grieve the Holy Spirit when we choose, knowingly and willingly, to *sin*.

Q2. What does it mean to quench the Holy Spirit?

A2. We quench the Spirit when we fail to *yield* to His leading in our lives.

Q3. What does it mean to walk in the Spirit?

A3. We walk in the Spirit when we consciously and prayerfully focus on the potential of the Holy Spirit's convicting, illuminating, leading, or enabling ministry coming to us at any moment, and keep ourselves *prepared* to follow and obey.

Chapter 11

Q1. What is the fruit of the Spirit?

A1. The fruit of the Spirit are character qualities that God possesses and that the Holy Spirit *imparts* to us as we live in trusting obedience to Jesus.

Q2. What is love?

A2. Love is the steady direction of our *will* toward the lasting good of another.

Q3. What is joy?

A3. Joy is a deep sense of *well-being* that is not dependent upon favorable circumstances, but rooted in a fundamental acceptance of, and confidence in, the will of God.

Q4. What is peace?

A4. Peace is the absence of anxiety and the presence of trusting assurance in the *promises* of God.

Chapter 12

Q1. What is patience?

A1. Patience is the ability to *endure* unpleasant people or circumstances for a higher cause.

Q2. What is kindness?

A2. Kindness is treating others *well* in word and deed.

Q3. What is goodness?

A3. Goodness is doing that which is *beneficial* for others.

Q4. What is faithfulness?

A4. Faithfulness is being *reliable* in doing what you should do.

Q5. What is gentleness?

A5. Gentleness is treating others *carefully*, with respect and sensitivity.

Q6. What is self-control?

A6. Self-control is the ability to resist immediate *gratification* for the sake of a higher goal.

About the Author

Max Anders is a pastor at heart who applies the truths of God's word to people's everyday lives. An original team member with Walk Thru the Bible Ministries and pastor of a mega-church for a number of years before beginning his speaking and writing ministry, Max has traveled extensively, speaking to thousands across the country.

His books include *30 Days to Understanding the Bible, 30 Days to Understanding How to Live a Christian Life, 30 Days to Understanding What Christians Believe.* He holds a Master of Theology degree from Dallas Theological Seminary and a doctorate from Western Seminary in Portland, Oregon.

If you are interested in having Max Anders speak at your conference, church, or special event, please call interAct Speaker's Bureau at 1-800-370-9932.